AF616762

SOUL UNSHACKLED

A harrowing and heroic autobiographical account of a prisoner

Sohail Fida

Edited by Hadi Rizvi

Paramount Publishing Enterprise

Karachi - Lahore - Islamabad - Faisalabad - Peshawar

SOUL UNSHACKLED

by

Sohail Fida

Edited by Hadi Rizvi

Published by

Paramount Publishing Enterprise

152/O, Block-2, P.E.C.H.S., Karachi-75400, Pakistan
Tel: 34310030, Fax: 34553772, E-mail: paramount@cyber.net.pk
Website: www.paramountbooks.com.pk

ISBN: 978-969-494-852-2

Printed in Pakistan

PUBLISHER'S NOTE

Why a Publisher's Note? Readers know that they seldom come across this type of preliminary writing when they go through the first few pages of a book. Like most publishers I prefer to remain inconspicuous, while working behind the scene to make sure that books of quality and substance are published in succession. This attitude allows the publishers the luxury of basking in their own feelings of self-fulfilment in relative privacy.

This work of autobiographical writing by Sohail Fida is of special significance to me for I doubt if I will ever get another opportunity to publish such an exceptional publication. *Soul Unshackled* has not come about by design on the part of either the author or the publisher. There is an aura of pre-destination about it.

Four years ago when we, at Paramount, decided to send a complimentary copy of our book *Memories and Reflections of a Pakistani Diplomat* by Sultan Muhammad Khan to Sohail on his request, we did not have the faintest idea that his plight and his gripping narrative would result in a book which we will hopefully cherish for a long time. Sohail did not have a clue either.

As a young and sensitive individual caught in a hard and challenging situation, Sohail Fida has achieved something truly unique. His book conveys an important message to Pakistan's younger generations which, if spread far and wide, has the potential to motivate them in turning the tables and make Pakistan what it was meant to be — a prosperous, tolerant and dignified country.

Soul Unshackled will make publishing history if we will be able to launch it on the premises of the jail, where Sohail is imprisoned. The event will in all probability be the first of its kind for we haven't been able to find out if in the past a book, written by a prisoner, was ever launched in the place of his imprisonment.

The book is planned to be published simultaneously in Urdu, Pashto, and English.

Iqbal Saleh Muhammad
Publisher

CONTENTS

FOREWORD

The lotus is considered to be one of the most magnificent and beautiful of all flowers in the world. However, it grows only in the stickiest, slimiest, and dirtiest of swamps. Similarly, sometimes in life the most positive things emerge out of the darkest and most negative of situations. Sohail Fida's story is one such example.

Falsely accused of murder as a young teenager and sentenced to death, Sohail's life took an unexpected turn from being a free and happy-go-lucky soul to being violated and becoming a victim of police brutality, as he was forced to live an animal-like life in the dark dungeons of prison.

Being young and impressionable, I can only imagine it to be a nightmare for any parent to watch their child go to prison and be surrounded by criminals on death row. Ordinarily, one would easily expect someone young in such a situation to be angry, have feelings of revenge or bitterness against the world, or at least expect their spirits to be crushed or crippled. Some may indulge in drugs or other bad habits or break into fights and join gangs within the prison.

Instead, what makes Sohail and his story so unique is that he stood his family proud. He dug deep inside to collect whatever strength he had within to come out victorious and blossom like a lotus when he was surrounded by nothing but quicksand. Without a speck of bitterness, anger or revenge, Sohail had the maturity to realize that he was going through this phase of his life for a reason. He knew that a Higher Power had chosen him as an example and an inspiration to prove to the world that the human spirit was far more capable of just spitting poison when bitten by a snake.

Sohail calmly continued with his studies and went on to do double Masters in prison and in return becoming a teacher and a mentor among his inmates. He is probably one of the very few prisoners to have achieved this mark which makes his story all the more praiseworthy.

I feel honored to have played a small role in bringing Sohail and his story to the limelight. As General Manager at Paramount at the time, I first received his letter in 2007 in which he had requested me for a book as a reference for his exams. I started corresponding with him and found out more about his story. Soon I was compelled to share it with the world and so I wrote an article about him in the newspaper. Shortly after, his death sentence was pardoned into a life sentence.

Sohail and I have been in touch ever since. We often exchange letters and he continues to be an inspiration to me. He always seems content and grateful, and never seems to complain about anything, which in turn often puts me to shame. I once tried to visit him, but he stopped me from making that visit as he did not want to meet me from behind bars. I cannot wait for the day he is released so I may at last embrace and welcome him as a free citizen again.

I am positive of Sohail's innocence, but I believe his experience in prison was not a waste. This book is a result of that experience which I hope will prove to be a voice for many other victims like Sohail across various prisons in the country. Sohail is lucky enough to have been released while he is still young. There are many others who will probably not be as lucky.

I hope that the luggage of Sohail's past only proves to be a stepping stone on the way of his progress instead of being a hurdle and that he makes use of this opportunity to the fullest.

I wish Sohail all possible health, happiness and success; and pray that he achieves whatever he strives for in life.

May Allah bless and protect us all.

With all the best wishes,

Muhammad Ali Khan

Former General Manager

Publishing and School Division

Paramount Publishing Enterprise

ACKNOWLEDGEMENT

I dedicate this book to Muhammad Ali Khan, Qudsia Kadri, and Amir Ali Shah.

The most wonderful things in life happen unexpectedly. It is nothing short of a miracle how a letter to a publishing company, Paramount Publishing Enterprise, requesting for a free book, turned my whole life's orientation towards the fulfillment of a dream.

It was because of Muhammad Ali Khan, Qudsia Kadri and Amir Ali Shah that I saw the light at the end of the gloomy tunnel of my life. It was because of these three, that I have received encouragement and love from caring people across of the country.

A long time ago I had read Paulo Coelho's *Alchemist* and since then it has become one of my favorite books. But I have since seen and met the real alchemists who guided and helped me in the right direction. Words alone cannot express the gratitude that I owe the following people for their caring concern and encouragement:

(Late) Abdul Akbar Khan, Adeeb Fatima Qureshi, Ashraf

Ahmad Ali, Ambassador Sultan Muhammad Khan, Amna Piracha, Asma Sahar, Asma Shah, Asim Khaliq, Atiya Siraj Munir, Amir Faraz, Brig. Rao Abid Hamid, Col. Ayaz M. Bashir, Col. Arshad Durrani, Col. Saadat Mehdi Khan, Dr. Asif Faruqi, Dr. Asif Mahmood Jan, Dr. Manzar Hassan, Dr. Zeba Aziz, Faiza Batool, Fouz Khalid Khan, Gen. Mirza Aslam Beg and his team, Haseeb Khalid Khan, Humair Awan, Idrees Sarwar Awan, Irfan Ahmad Khan, Khurshid Hadi, Maria Pervaiz, Misbah Khalid, Masroor Ahmad, M. Aziz Haji Dossa, Muhammad Rafiq, Navid Ahmad, Nadia Ali Khan, Nighat Waheed, Nusrat Lashari, P. Harimohan, Sherin Masud Khadarposh, Sher Bahadur Afridi, Syed Ali Mujtaba, S. Fida Yunus, Syed Azmat Hassan, Tanveer Jahan, Urdu Bazaar publishers, Wahab, Yassir Mahmood, Zahar Marwat and Zahid Kazmi.

I would particularly like to thank the publisher, Mr. Iqbal Saleh Muhammad, for giving me the opportunity to relive all those moments. I am highly beholden to my parents, whose love for me has been like the sunshine in the valley and the rain in the desert. I am most grateful to my cousin Rafiq, who has always helped and oversaw my writings with friendship, charm, and humor, and who read several of my sections and gave me sound advice.

PROLOGUE

It is said, 'When the going gets tough, the tough get going'. For Sohail Fida, the going did not just get tough, it got the toughest. His story is the stuff that we find in legends, folklore or fiction. But this is neither myth nor fiction. It is a true story of a 17-year-old from a small town in Swat, in the Northern regions of Pakistan. It carries the most profound lessons of courage, determination, resilience and above all, of faith and character. It stirs the deepest chords of conscience even in the most insensitive heart. A person does not deserve to be called a human being if he is not empathically touched by the ordeal of this young man, and how he reacted while undergoing it.

Wrongfully framed, inhumanly tortured to the limits of submission, then duped into a confession on the promise of a compromise, Sohail Fida was convicted of murder and sentenced to death. For any person, especially one in his youthful teens, the tragic turn of events would have numbed the brain, or led to insanity or violence. The least one could have expected is a revengeful bitterness against the system of justice and society in general. But amazingly, adversity brought out the most sublime human qualities in Sohail Fida. Credit for these qualities must also be given to his family, who must have surely ingrained these values during his formative years.

Before his arrest, Sohail Fida was like any other carefree youngster preferring sports and extra-curricular activities to studies. He attended school only in deference to the wishes of his family, especially his father. He himself says that when he decided to continue his studies in jail, it was only to please his father. Nevertheless, even this thought is a tribute to his upbringing.

All along as he narrates his account of the years in jail and on 'Death Row', he has a special place in his heart and mind for all who had been helpful or had shown just a hint of kindness to him. Even when he talks about the beatings and abuses, there is no bitterness in mind or attitude. It is more like a matter of fact mention and nothing more. He has gratefully acknowledged each person by name and deed that helped him in the pursuit of his studies, encouraged his perseverance or just did not create any hindrances in his endeavors.

Today, Sohail Fida's death sentence has been commuted to life imprisonment, and while he is anxious to get back to freedom and family, he wonders how he will cope with his new life. He believes that it was because of being locked up in jail that he managed to study and complete a twin Master's, one in International Relations, and one in History. He is sure but for the jail, he would have at the most attained a Bachelor's Degree and that too at the behest of his father's wishes.

For a person who had hardly any exposure to the English language, to write about his life in jail with such fluency, feelings and clarity of thought, is indeed remarkable. We have made no changes except for some editorial amendments or typos in the story of Sohail Fida. It is his own story written in his own style and words. It leaves the reader emotionally distraught; and yet it has no complains, nor self-pity. It is a story of unprecedented accomplishments, despite the extreme emotional, psychological and physical trauma. In fact as one reads through it, one feels that these very conditions spurred this young man to excel, both as a scholar and as a human being.

Through his story of perseverance and accomplishment, and the positive contribution towards his achievements by all who helped him, we want the world to know that there are people in this part of the world, who despite all the hardships, poverty and the more recently generalized stigma of terrorism and fanaticism; observe, follow and practice basic human values. The encouragement given to Sohail Fida, by the jail wardens, superintendents, university professors and so many more, is indeed unique, exemplary, and highly praiseworthy. There is no example where a convict on 'Death Row' in any country has accomplished the feat of attaining a Master's Degree, let alone two. Surely his accomplishment deserves wide recognition and public acclaim international fame; inclusion in the Guinness Book of World Records; and much more to serve as a beacon of light to all humans, especially those facing adversity and misfortune.

Wing Commander (Retired) Hadi Rizvi
Pakistan Air Force

Take care of your Thoughts

Because they become Words.

Take care of your Words

Because they become Actions.

Take care of your Actions

Because they become Habits.

Take care of your Habits

Because they become Character.

Take care of your Character

Because it becomes your Destiny.

And your Destiny will be your Life...

And there is no religion higher than the Truth.

— *Hadi Rizvi*

CHAPTER 1

HOW I CAME TO WRITE MY STORY

"No man seeking a goal ever complains of want of opportunity."

On 15th of October 2007, I received a letter from Qudsia Kadri, Editor-in-Chief of the Financial Post, expressing the wish to publish a series of articles on the story of my life. I was too excited to sit still and started pacing the barrack even though it was not big enough for any kind of walking. But in my mind and soul, I felt as if I was in the valley of Bahrain in Swat. I have always had the dream of writing the story of my life; I always wanted to be a writer, but was not sure if my dream would ever come true. I knew that if I worked hard enough, there would be a possibility that I could achieve my dream. This request by the *Financial Post* gave me the first step towards my desire. People can take away many things from me, like my money, my books, my personal letters, even my freedom, but I will not let them take away my dreams. Dreams without a vision are mere wishes. One has to take action to turn a dream into reality.

I was unsure where to start from: my early childhood or from the day I landed in jail. I wrote to Qudsia Kadri for some advice. She suggested starting from my early life. So I started writing and in a short time sent in my first episode by registered mail, thinking that I will receive some alteration and recommendations from the newspaper. I soon received a reply and was both excited and worried when I opened the letter. Excited because they had published the first episode without any corrections; and worried because I had not yet started on the second episode. I immediately got down to writing and surprisingly made good progress. However, by the time I was through with the fifth episode, there was some disturbance in the jail. There was protest and mass demonstration by the lawyers in the country against President General Pervez Musharraf for firing Chief Justice Iftikhar Muhammad Choudhry. There were many arrests and to make room for the lawyers in detention, the entire Juvenile Sector was cramped into a single barrack in Sector 4. I managed to continue my work even under these circumstances.

While I was into the final episode, my father wrote to me that my niece, Sarah, somehow got to know that I was a prisoner in jail and not in any university where she had been told I was. This was a big shock to me because I loved her very much and now I was not sure what she will think of me. I asked my father about Sarah's reaction on learning the truth about me. She had found this out when my father took a copy of the *Financial Post* to my brother-in-law with my article in it. The last time I saw

Sarah, she was four years old and I had gone from jail to the examination hall in Swat. In her innocence she had asked her mother about the big bangles I was wearing — referring to the handcuffs. Often I had wondered what Sarah will think about her *Mamoo Jan* (Maternal Uncle) when she came to know the truth about my position, that in the eyes of the society I was a thief and a murderer. She had decided to come and see me and I was, both anxiously and apprehensively, looking forward to her visit. Eventually the day came and we met. It was a long time since we had seen each other and we both experienced shyness and awkwardness as we met. I could not think of what to say and ended up asking clumsy questions about her school. She had brought along some fruits and a cream cake for me. The meeting ended on a quiet note. She unexpectedly came to see me again the very next week and this time with her parents. This visit went off better than the last one and we talked more freely about many topics. She read out a poem and an essay she had written in English and I was surprised at how well she wrote at an age when I was barely beginning to learn Urdu. I was told that when my sister prepared food for me, Sarah insisted on helping her saying that *Mamoo Jan* would also taste her love in the food. She has also started regularly writing to me now. I was very happy that she did not reject me after knowing my situation. Motivated by this happiness I continued to write my final episode with much enthusiasm. On the eve of Eid, I gave final touches to my last episode for the *Financial Post*, letting out a big sigh of relief followed by a satisfactory smile. Just before going to sleep, I pictured all the naysayers who had cautioned me against chasing my dreams.

By the time my story came out in print, I became somewhat

popular and received visits from a number of Federal and Provincial Ministers and NGO representatives. I could not stop myself from thinking that for some I was just a show piece. An inaugural ceremony would take place whenever any VIP would come to meet me.

During December 2008, I was summoned to the Superintendent's Office and on my reaching it, I was scolded by the Personal Attendant of the Superintendent as to why I had shown up in sandals. He sent me running to get dressed up appropriately because someone from Islamabad, the capital, was coming to interview me. After about twenty minutes of trying to find something presentable to wear (all my clothes were up for washing), I managed to borrow the most decent available in the Juvenile Sector, and returned to the Office. To my surprise, I saw the Office set up with cameras and lights. I was greeted by Shehryar Mufti of *Dawn News*, who conducted my interview. I was quite nervous with all, the equipment, and to top it all the Superintendent with his staff was in attendance with the host. Slowly the nervousness subsided as I focused on the questions being asked. Barrister Shahida Jamil, the Federal Minister for Social Welfare and Special Education had also come along with Mr. Shehryar Mufti. With her I discussed the state of the Juvenile Library and Computer Center. She offered a lot of assistance and donated a 26 inch Television for the Computer Center. She came a few more times and one of her visits coincided with that of my family. She was gracious enough to meet with them.

Before the next visit of Barrister Shahida Jamil, I met with Mr. Ansar Burney, who was the Federal Minister for Human Rights and the Head of the Ansar Burney Trust. He offered me a position upon my release and the promise to send me abroad for further education. He also said that if the opponent party was willing to settle the case through a monetary compromise, he would come up with the money, no matter how much. He mentioned all this in his address to the Juvenile Prisoners. I considered his offer sincere and hold him in high esteem, but this did not move me as much as the motherly love of Barrister Shahida Jamil. She had patted my shoulder and face and said, "Son, do not give up." That affection is fresh even today.

I got my first salary from Jail School late at night in December 2007. I held the salary envelope and moved it around in my hand, swaying it again and again in front of my eyes. I was thinking about whom I must send it. There were many alchemists in my life, who were like shining stars in the open seas, and who had helped and guided me in the right direction. I thought that it would be a good gesture to donate my first salary to one of them. I remembered a dream in which I saw myself as a lecturer, and presented my first salary to my grandfather, who felt very proud of his grandson. I then sent a money order and a registered letter to him in deference to my dream. I had not yet learnt that my grandfather — or Daaji — had passed away exactly forty days after my grandmother had died. My mother received the letter and distributed the money among the poor. I eventually heard about his death from a person from my home town. It was an absolute shock and I felt that somebody had given me a giant kick in the head. Daaji's death had hit me like nothing else I had experienced before and never want to experience again. I knew that Daaji was suffering a great deal of pain from various ailments but had no idea that these were life threatening. Suddenly I realized that I had not seen Daaji for a long time and now there was no chance to talk to him. I mourned him deeply. I love my parents very much, but loved Daaji above all. I remember an incident when I said this to him in front of my parents and he was so touched that he cried. We were lucky to have him as our pillar and our stronghold.

There are times in one's life when one cannot imagine how to cope with some incident but somehow the time passes and we manage to survive through it. On hearing about Daaji's death I felt a strange emptiness but curiously a little stronger. I started to see all the similarities I had with him and started to draw strength from it. My grandfather was no more in this world, but I now feel that I am becoming Daaji. Sometimes it feels that his words are coming from my lips. I miss him a lot and I want him to know that his grandson will not disappoint him. I will try my best to reach my potential by learning more and eventually contribute positively to the society.

In January 2008, a batch of foreign prisoners was transferred from Peshawar to Haripur Central Jail. They were assigned to stay in the first barrack of the Juvenile Sector. I met Hendrik on the second day of their arrival. Hendrik was one of the few prisoners who could speak English. He would join us for small talk and his main subjects of discussion were current affairs and philosophy. I showed him some of my books and since he liked them I loaned him two of my favorites, namely, *The Little Prince* by Antoine de Saint and *The Picture of Dorian Gray* by Oscar Wilde. He returned the favor by lending me one of his favorites, *Crime and Punishment* by Fyodor Dostoevsky. He also introduced me to the great classics of Russian literature.

On Hendrik's advice, I sent an application with all the supporting documents to the Home Department of NWFP (North West Frontier Province, now known as Khyber Pakhtunkhwa) for granting me a better class in prison. I had become entitled to this privilege after completing my Masters Degree. The application went through the normal red tape but was finally approved by the District Officer, Revenue and Estate Collection of Swat and returned to the Home Department. For no stated reason, the Home Department turned down the application. After that, Brig. Rao Abid Hamid (of Human Rights Commission of Pakistan (HRCP)) and Barrister Shahida Jamil re-applied on my behalf. The case was reopened and reprocessed, but once again rejected by the Home Department. My father decided to pursue this on his own and approached the Home Department. Meanwhile, three Home Secretaries were replaced and now there was a lady in place. Qudsia Kadri, of the Frontier Post spoke for me and somehow I felt that this time it would be approved. My feeling proved to be correct and finally my case for a higher class in jail was approved on 15th of May 2008. On first June, the Central Prison in Haripur received the approval and I was moved to Cell 11 in 'B' class. Ironically from this cell I could look directly into the back of my former Death Row cell, which served as a permanent reminder of where I had been.

The cells of 'B' class are identical to the ones on Death Row but the life style and regulations are very different. A gas fitted kitchen with a cook is available for each 'B' Class resident prisoner. Another benefit is the weekly dry and wet ration such as meat, eggs, wheat, pulse, vegetables, condiments, cooking oil, milk, tea and sugar, delivered to the prisoners of this class. This is definitely a more comfortable living area for the prisoners. Another luxury that I now enjoyed was a bed, two chairs and a table in my cell. These were the things I had been deprived of for about nine years. I don't think that anyone who ever booked into a luxury hotel ever enjoyed that comfort as much as I valued these.

I was hesitant to take a cook. I had seen many of the other 'B' class prisoners bossing their cooks around and I could not see myself in such a position of assumed authority. When I lived in the Juvenile sector, I was in a group with my cousin Rafiq and friends sharing all the duties. Now it was my responsibility of cooking, cleaning and washing alone. 'B' Class residents are not supposed to receive food from the Jail Mess called *Jail Lungar*. However, when ration was doubled and the food standard became better, I started to receive food from the Lungar. I was afraid that the other 'B' Class residents would consider it poor man's food and make fun of me. But after continuing like this for a while, I was praised for my independence, especially by those residents who had constant arguments with their cooks.

When I was in the Juvenile sector, I was not allowed to go to other sectors without the permission of the Chief Warden. A numberdar was posted at the gate to make sure that no one entered or went without permission. An older prisoner was also appointed as a guardian (known as 'Baba') who takes care of the needs of the juvenile prisoners. This included fetching items from the shop on our behalf and escorting to the visitor's room. For Rafiq and myself, it was strange to be treated as adults for five years on death row and then suddenly to be treated like children in the juvenile sector. Now I was happy that I could freely go to the other jail sectors.

Hendrik would come over at 2 p.m. after finishing his assigned duty at the factory and then Rafiq would also join us. We used to discuss various topics till closing time. Our topics ranged from religion to whether America was justified in occupying Afghanistan and Iraq. Hendrik would contribute a lot of interesting ideas, especially related to philosophy. The study of philosophy had dramatically changed my way of thinking about the world and its working. Philosophy to me is the greatest form of thinking; something that gets our mind to work and makes us more aware of the world. Philosophy taught me that everything in life can not be seen as good or bad, or black and white, but that there are other shades as well. For instance, I have seen people who walk so carefully so as to not tread over an ant, yet often boast how they killed their enemies in cold blood. Sometimes, Hendrik and Rafiq were stopped at the gate by the numberdar or the Chief Warden would not permit them to come to 'B' Class which would frustrate them and leave me bored waiting for the next discussion.

'B' Class greatly helped in my study environment. Studying for my Masters in History on a chair was a pleasure in itself. The exams were to be held in August 2008, which was just a few weeks away. By the University regulations, I was to attempt five papers out of a total of seven, followed by a Viva Voce. I had done quite well and was sure of passing till something unexpected came up. A new examiner came and told me to appear in the sixth paper. I objected by telling him that I had already done five as was required by the rules. The sixth paper was History of India after 1947. But the examiner would not agree and got in touch with the Hall Superintendent for confirmation. I was told that this paper was mandatory along with another which followed in two days and had to be taken by me. I was told that if I did not take these I would be marked absent which would result in a failing grade. The thought of failing in the exam made me think twice as I would embarrass a lot of people who were supporting me, especially my family and my Alchemists. I realized that an argument at this stage would not improve my situation so I submitted and sat for the papers. Luckily, the papers were not difficult and dealt with a lot of material which I had studied in the International Relations examination. I confidently completed four out of five questions that needed to be done and later did well in the Viva Voce also. One day before the result came out I received a letter from the Hazara University which read:

> *It is to inform that the candidate concerned has been appeared in MA History (Final) Annual Examination 2008 and attempted seven papers instead of five papers, wasting University precious time as well as documents. His case has been placed before the University Discipline Committee for further decision. He will appear before the committee for his justification etc. as and when call letter will issued to him.*
>
> *S/d. Controller Examination Hazara University*

In January 2009, Assistant Controller of Examination came to interview me. I gave my reasons for the misunderstanding about the papers. He listened attentively but in the end I could not judge his response and he left me in suspense. After a week my result was announced and to my pleasant surprise I had scored 5th position in the Board. The news of my MA (History) result spread quickly and was published in many newspapers. Following this, I was visited by the sub-editor and the crime reporter of the *Daily Mashriq*. I met them in the office of the Superintendent. The sub-editor showed me some of my articles that were published in the *Dawn* and *Financial Post* and wanted my permission to have them translated in Urdu for his newspaper. I first gave him the permission but later changed my mind and consented to translate them myself for fear that some of the portions may be taken out of context. My family later told me that my articles were well liked by many people; especially the Internally Displaced Persons (IDPs) of Swat. I also received direct letters of praise from some IDPs.

Due to the militancy in Swat, things started to deteriorate rapidly and many public executions were carried out, where people had their throats slit and many were left hanging in public places to intimidate the residents. A lot of this happened in the Green Square near my home. At the same time, the militants started blowing up schools. One school near our house was blown up in the middle of the night and the huge explosion even damaged our home. One of our petrol pumps was also damaged due to shelling by the militants. My father's car was stolen during this period. This deteriorating law and order situation allowed a dramatic rise in crime in the area — a phenomena previously unheard of in Swat and its surroundings.

My family did not tell me all that was happening for fear that it might unnecessarily upset me. I used to regularly phone them from the jail's PCO (Public Call Office). The provincial government had opened PCOs in the NWFP Central and District prisons in 2008, but in October 2009, all PCOs were closed by the IG Prisons as they were being used by the detained Taliban. Sometimes through the news, I would learn about what was going on in my area and this was a cause of grave concern to me. It eventually got so unsafe that my family fled to Charsadda. Everyone was prepared to take whatever jobs they could find in other parts of the country just to get away from all the bloodshed. When the writ of the government was restored in Swat, my family returned to their home after a four-month exile in Charsadda.

The first of June 2009 was a very happy day for all prisoners because the Supreme Court of Pakistan passed a historical judgment about remissions. Most important in that were the restoration of under-trial remissions, which gave me a benefit of six years on one count. Second part of that judgment was about concurrent sentences. We pursued that in the Federal Sharia Court to seek concurrent running of sentences awarded to us on both counts i.e. sentence of imprisonment for life (25 years) under Section 302 and five years under Section 380 (theft). But, unfortunately our application was turned down on 17th May 2010. I will be released within ten months from now taking in account the various remissions granted to prisoners by the President, Chief Minister, IG (Inspector General) Prisons and credit gained for acquiring educational qualifications.

I have seen death closely for five years and did not even spend a single night without thinking about it. To fear death is to ignore life and all the beautiful and wonderful things that life has to offer. Life is not about dying. It is about living and accomplishing everything that we can. If we fear death instead of accepting it, we will never live our lives to its fullest. We need to learn to appreciate life and everything that surrounds us. I do not fear death itself but do not want to die with a rope around my neck. Having experienced the joys of life and its pleasures once, I fear the death cell. I am sometimes seized by the fear that this dream may end as suddenly as it started. I have come to love God for the mysterious ways His hand moves. I request Him to make pleasant the remaining surprises of my life. I believe that the beauty of life can be best understood by loving and enjoying the small things.

Citing my own example, I can safely say that my life is a living proof that anything may happen to anybody at anytime, and that miracles still happen, except that we tend to overlook them. Everyone has dreams which can be turned into reality and there are other hopes that we know are impossible to attain, but we still create a dream world to escape from realities. It is purely for their entertainment value that dreams are the greatest gifts the humans are blessed with. Miracles are the happenings of events which we can never think to dream of. There is a very long list of people who played a part in changing my life for the better but I am most grateful to the jail.

Thank you jail for providing excellent educational facilities. The accommodation wasn't bad either. You taught me to take pleasure in the small things of life. Because of you I have met and come into contact with wonderful, kind-hearted and real human beings and I am still enjoying the show. I request you to please let me go now so that I can start my third life and write the final chapter of my book.

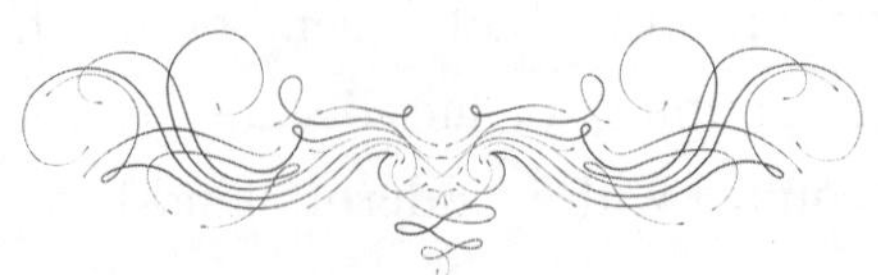

CHAPTER 2

EARLY YEARS

"Every story has an end, but in life every ending is just a new beginning."

I was born in Peshawar on the 28th of August 1982, along with my twin sister Gulalai. My family has lived in Swat from as far back as anyone can remember. Our family doctor in Mingora, my hometown in Swat, expected a complicated birth and referred my mother to the Lady Reading Hospital in Peshawar. The Lady Reading Hospital had more modern facilities and a concentration of specialist doctors. Peshawar is the capital city of the NWFP (North Western Frontier Province), so named during the British Raj over India. It has been renamed as Khyber Pakhtunkhwa. Because we were both weak and delicate babies, we spent sometime in the incubator. My mother was discharged after a month and the family returned to Mingora. However, Gulalai's health took a turn for the worst and she died within four months.

Of late, Swat has been in the news for all the wrong reasons. As I remember, it was a serene and tranquil area of peace-loving people, where everybody kept to himself. The people were religiously inclined but without any hint of extremism. *Mullahs* (Clerics) were confined to mosques, leading prayers and delivering Friday sermons. It was so peaceful that women, in case of emergency, could leave their homes even in the middle of the night. Even though the number of women pursuing higher education was considerably less than men, yet most of them did receive at least a primary education. *"Purdah"* and *"Burqah"* (local terms for 'the act of veiling by women') were matters of choice, not compulsion, and those who did not cover their faces were accorded the same respect. It was famous for tourism in contrast to today's terrorism.

Before partition, Swat was a princely state ruled by the Wali-e-Swat. Unlike what has been reported about the rulers of other princely states, the Wali-e-Swat was and is still respected for taking a keen interest in the socio-economic welfare of the subjects and developing the infrastructure of the state. He took special interest in promoting education and establishing a whole network of schools and the very beautiful Jehanzeb College. It is mainly due to his efforts that Swat has a relatively high literacy rate. As a youngster, I remember that I seldom met a person who could not at least read and write. People were broad-minded. I sometimes wonder as to where from all these ill-educated and misinformed mullahs have cropped up.

According to the practice of the time, my father married when he was still studying for his graduation. He was the brightest and the most hard working of all his brothers. My grandfather asked him to give up further education and join him in business as soon as he completed his graduation.

My father was the first person in the family to have studied upto graduation. He always lamented the fact that he was deprived of the chance to study further. He would have preferred to be a professor rather than running the business, even if it meant being poorer than he is. He took great interest in our education. My mother was educated till 8th Class. She gave us religious education at home. She taught us the Quran, *Namaz* (Islamic Prayer) and the basic tenets of Islam. She had devised a clever way to ensure our full concentration on the subjects. There was a well that we could see from where we sat. She would cover that with a blanket and lay an axe alongside it when we were not looking. This was her monster who would take us away if we did not pay attention to the lesson. Before the lesson would end, she had arranged for the veil to be cleared by one of our aunts. We, of course, did not know all this at that time.

In our house, education was a top priority. My father always wanted us to stand out as good examples in the neighbourhood. When I was six years old, my father admitted me in a school near our house, where my elder sister Salma was also studying. I attended this school till the second class. When my father felt that the school was losing standard, he moved me to International Education Public School and College, where I studied till Matriculation (10th year of Education). My father was a regular visitor to the school and would constantly check on my progress. In order to improve our formal writing and expression, my father would have us write applications for whatever we required. None of our applications were ever rejected. In fact the only application that was turned down was my request for a cassette recorder with remarks that at age fourteen I did not need one and I would not be able to maintain it properly as yet. The added remarks were very interesting. It was written that although a cassette recorder costs only 700 rupees, a request for books costing 7,000 rupees would not have been rejected.

Although my mother tongue is Pashto, we were encouraged to speak Urdu, so as to do better in school. At home, my mother and later my elder sister would help me with my homework. As we grew older, my father hired tutors to help us with mathematics and science in the afternoon after school. I also received religious education, mainly reading the Quran from an elderly neighbor, whom we called Mullah Aabay. Every Friday was family get-together day, when my aunts and the cousins would come over to our house and we partied till dinner, watched movies and generally gossiped.

Despite all the efforts of my family, I remained at best an average student. My interest was taken up more by sports (like badminton, cricket, biking), music, and video games. I started reading the children's and other magazines only after I landed in jail and had nothing else to do. The most painful event of my school life was my 7th class result. I had passed with far lesser marks than the expectations of my father. I then committed a blunder and tried to tamper with the results, and did it so clumsily that as soon as my father had one look at it, and his face turned pale. He had never hit me in my life, but the words he spoke haunt me till today. "What will the principal and your teachers think? That Fida Hussain's son is a cheat," he said.

When I was arrested the first thought that came to my mind was, what will the people say? That Fida Hussain's son is a murderer! It was not the police torture and humiliation but just this thought which still cuts through my heart like a knife. My younger brother once on a visit to my cell confided in me that he had tried the same trick on papa a couple of times and got away with it. Some people are just plain unlucky and never get away with mistakes and blunders. I think I am one of them. Having learnt a harsh lesson, I wholeheartedly (or at least tried to) study for the Matriculation exam. And, it is perhaps the day when my examination result was declared which is most cherished in the memory of my early life. It was also the last time I would see my father so happy. I will never forget his beaming smile, which lit up as he took my face in his hands and said, "Sohail, I am proud of you." I had secured only slightly more than average marks but was of course overjoyed both for making my father happy and the CD player which he had promised to buy me, if I scored good marks.

It was the love of my father and not wanting to disappoint him that made me study hard enough and I never failed a single exam, quite an achievement considering my lack of intellectual capabilities and my interest in extracurricular activities.

The biggest influence in my early life was that of Daaji, my grandfather (May Allah Almighty give him a long and happy life). He is a self-made person and a successful businessman of his time. Apart from my great-grandfather's clothing business, where my grandfather first started to work, he indulged in other ventures as well. He started traveling to India from where he would purchase wholesale goods that were not available in Swat. Thus, he started his new career as a goods transporter (used to transport goods from one place to another on mules). In one of his trips, he bought lanterns which would light up with kerosene oil. For advertising, he hired a mule driver and a crier who went around beating a drum and shouting, "Come see the new invention to light your nights like the sun." My great uncle was lured by the 'Shell Kerosene' success and wanted to do the same business but my grandfather convinced him not to do so in Mingora but in Mardan, a city some distance away. This he advised will avoid competition. Through sheer determination and hard work he became a successful businessman and established Swat's first petrol filling station before Partition. My grandfather was a devout Muslim and offered the five obligatory prayers without failing. To win his favor, I would accompany him to the mosque but sneak out the minute he started his prayers, only to return when he was about to finish. I was not only showered with sweets and other favors, but also held as an example of a dutiful and devoted grandson. My cousin Rafiq knew about my ploy and would at times threaten to expose the real me, but I would quieten him by sharing some of the goodies I received from my grandfather. In fact not just we children, some of the older ones also took part in such antics. I know this because sometimes I would see one of my uncles roaming around in the bazaar outside the mosque and we would pretend that we did not see each other. At another time when I saw my uncle rushing towards the mosque thinking he was late and therefore would be scolded by my grandfather, I told him that Daaji was not well and so did not come to the mosque. On hearing this my uncle returned to his home. Daaji partially retired after fulfilling his ambition of constructing a filling station for each of his sons. Despite being retired from business and at the ripe age of 80, he was a daily visitor to our filling station. He was honest to the core and would himself personally check the filling station to make sure no tampering had been done with meters and pumps. I liked him most, because he did not lay great stress on education as my father did. He often joked with my father. "Don't try to make my eldest grandson a bookworm. Let him also learn about the business." He said, it was after all due to business that we were getting education in good schools. Often my grandfather would take me along to the station and tell me how he had started the business and how the pumps were manually operated when he first set up the filling station. I would help him out with his accounting registers and daily logs and read the newspaper to him. He himself could read and despite his age, he had excellent eyesight but he just liked me to do it because I was his favorite grandson.

He narrated a story that once when the car of the Wali-e-Sawat's friend had come to the village for the first time, the simple villagers placed grass and water in front of it. The Wali-e-Swat's friend's sawari (the innocent villagers were more familiar with horse or cattle drawn vehicles) must be hungry after a long journey, they thought. My grandfather of course was much wiser than them; he owned the first filling station established in the area.

Up to the date of my being sentenced to death, he enjoyed a robust health. During the trial of my case, my father and uncles kept him unaware of the date of my court hearings, thinking that he would not be able to bear the shock of seeing me handcuffed and in police custody. Still he managed to find out about my days of appearances in court a couple of times and came to reassure me that he was alive and though he may be old, but was still strong enough to get his grandson and heir out of jail.

I have not seen him for the past five years. His health started falling ever since I was sentenced to death. He had lost much of his eyesight and hearing and was almost bed-ridden.

In my death cell and now in the barrack, often late at night, I have wondered with a broken soul, how my father would have faced him that fateful day when I was sentenced to death.

I have been told that my grandfather blamed my father for failing to save my life. I wonder if he has forgiven him now that my death sentence has been commuted to life imprisonment.

CHAPTER 3

COLLEGE LIFE AND ARREST

"If God brings you to it,
He will bring you through it."

When it was time for admission to college, my father wanted me to join Islamia College, Peshawar, where he himself had graduated from. It is one of the most distinguished institutions and colleges of Khyber Pakhtunkhwa. But my mother opposed the idea saying that I was too young and would be unable to adjust in a big city away from home. Hence, my father left the choice to me. I decided on Jehanzeb College, Swat. It is a beautiful building and is named after the Wali-e-Swat, who constructed it in 1953. It is said that the design of the building and architecture is based on the style of an English college.

College brought a welcome change and greatly altered my life-style. No longer was it compulsory to attend each and every class. I had a lot more freedom and instead of just playing video games and listening to music, other extra-curricular activities entered my life. In college there was more freedom. No more cane, no more uniform, no more orders and no more thought control. It was also the time when I saw my first movie in a cinema hall. It was when I learnt to beg for attendance. It was also when I learnt to take out my father's car without permission. There was a refreshing abandon about being in college. It was also the time of my first and last love for a girl who was studying in 10th Class. She was the daughter of my uncle who lived in Charsadda, a town some distance away from where we lived. We had gone to Charsadda and when we returned she came to Swat to her relatives with us. After a considerably long and hopeful waiting and exchange of looks, I managed to get my first letter across requesting her phone number. I was overjoyed on receiving her reply the next day. Making a call to her was another problem. Calling from my home was out of the question. Despite being very liberal my father was very conservative in such matters. He had given strict orders that I was not to look at girls and asked me as to how I would feel if somebody glared at my sister in a similar fashion. My friends introduced me to the owner of a PCO (Public Call Office), who charged double the rate for the call but asked no questions. Over the next few weeks, I would often spend hours on the phone with her. Talking to her on the phone made me feel a certain kind of happiness that I had never felt before. That small cabin with a wooden chair, a telephone whose numbers had faded with extensive use and a floor covered with cigarette butts was my wonderland. My whole life revolved around waiting for the appointed time of our phone conversations. I gifted her cassettes of Indian movies: *Dilwale Dulhaniya Laay Jaaingay, Hum Dil Day Chukkay Sanam, Dil Say,* and *Pardes*.

I also gave her my picture and she promised to give me hers, but before that promise could materialize I landed in jail. I am sure she would have been relieved that her picture did not fall into the hands of a criminal, a murderer.

My romantic life had a span of four months. The thought of those four months would surely haunt her as a nightmare, as she is happily married now, but for me those days remain like the memories of many blissful years when I knew no worries and everything appeared to be rose-colored.

My father owned a filling station near Bahrain, the most scenic valley of Swat. He also leased a house in the lush green valley with equally beautiful mountains, where we used to spend our holidays. Bahrain means two rivers and the name is appropriate because this is the place of confluence of two rivers. The weather is very pleasant here. In our younger days, my cousins and I used to enjoy throwing flat stones on the water and watch them go skimming several times over the surface. Just putting your feet in that pure and cool water was a blissful feeling.

One of my most strange memories is associated with a grave of a woman next to our filling station. The story was that when she was pregnant, she was murdered by her husband and her body was dumped. After her body was found, no one knew about her family, so my father along with some other people arranged her funeral and buried her next to the filling station. I was very touched by her story and often spent hours alongside her grave and especially on Eid days (days of Islamic festivities and reverence). I also started seeing her in my dreams. The strangest thing is that often in my dreams she would tell me about some of the future events in advance. I am not a superstitious person and I do not believe in things like magic and jinn or extra-terrestrial objects. I have also never been inclined towards mysticism or Sufism. But this is a phenomenon of my life that has remained unsolved till today. I wonder if it was a figment of my imagination or just another example of how the Beneficent Hand of Almighty Allah moves in strange ways. For some strange reason other people also started visiting her grave and would offer *Fatiha* (Quranic Prayer for the departed), and pray for the fulfillment of their wishes, as one would at the shrine of a saint. The mysterious and strange incident about her is that when her family learnt about her death and visited the grave, we found out that they were not from Swat. They told us that her name was Sohaila and this name is now inscribed on her tomb stone.

One day when I was returning from college I saw a bird-seller selling beautiful colored small birds. I bought three pairs and took them home. My grandfather admonished me saying that how would I have felt if God forbid I was imprisoned. I replied that I shall give them food, water, and shelter; and they were better off with me, where they have all the food they want and are safe from preying birds. Besides, I said that fish were never meant to be in a tank or the chickens in a farm. Sensing that I would not change my mind, my grandfather just shook his head saying, "Allah created birds to fly in the free air. Who are we to cage them? But you will never understand these things."

The second of April 2000 is the most fateful day of my life when my world turned upside down. Early in the morning I learnt the shocking news of the murder of my friend and cousin Zubair. He had been murdered by some unknown person/persons in mysterious circumstances. The fact of it being a blind murder was also mentioned in the First Information Report (FIR).

His younger brother was crying. He said while embracing me, "Sohail *lala* ('elder brother' in Pashto language), my Zubair *bhaijan* ('elder brother' in Urdu language) is dead." He was weeping uncontrollably and instead of consoling him I broke down into tears myself.

The dead body had been taken to the hospital for post mortem. How painful it must have been for a father to have an adult son murdered for no fault or reason and then have his body cut-up by the doctors. At that time I did not of course know what post mortem meant. When his body was returned, it had a big stitch which ran from the neck to the abdomen — the result of the post mortem.

I kept on thinking as to who would commit such a heinous crime and murder an innocent boy who was friendly with everybody he met, even strangers. May Allah Almighty rest his soul in peace and shower his grave with blessings. He certainly did not deserve to die, especially at such a young age.

During the funeral ceremony, I came to know that six people had been arrested on suspicion for involvement in the murder.

Later in the evening, I along with my cousin Rafiq was called to the Mingora Police Station. The police officials who sent for us said we were not being called due to any suspicion or as being suspects, but as friends of the deceased. They wanted to record our statements and perhaps that could shed some light on any possible motive a person may have had for murdering our friend.

When I was going to the police station, little did I know what fate had in store for me and that my college days and the dream of my teenage days was soon to be turned into a nightmare and I would wake to the harsh realities of the world.

CHAPTER 4

POLICE LOCK-UP, TORTURE, AND CONFESSION

"Constant dripping hollows out a stone."

My father took me (along with my best friend, cousin and co-accused Rafiq) to the police station. When we entered the police station, the officer in-charge of the police station (know as 'Station House Officer' or SHO) was very courteous and called us "sons" and my father "a brother". He apologized to my father for the inconvenience and said he wanted to inquire from us whether we had any knowledge of the deceased's enmity with anyone. He said that six persons were already under investigation as possible suspects. Then he took my father aside and when the SHO came back, his face was red with rage and he shouted to us, "You are sitting on the chairs like you are the sons of the Prime Minister, get up you criminals." He told his subordinates to throw us into the lockup.

Later, I learnt that the SHO had demanded Rs. 200,000 as gratification to set us free as we were according to him prime suspects, because of being good friends of the deceased. My father being unaware of how the justice system works in our country was outraged and an exchange of hot words took place between them. I wonder if my father feels his greed for the money is responsible for all the hardships me and my family subsequently faced. But I know it is not a matter of money. My father being a man of principles was, in fact, infuriated by the allegation that I could commit such a heinous crime.

This complete turn of events had simply devastated me. My mind went so numb. I did not even feel afraid. I was simply dumbfounded. After an hour or so my mind gradually started working and I started to feel the cold cemented floor of the lock-up. Evening turned into night and I began thinking that after recording my statement they'll let me go. I was emotionally so exhausted that I went to sleep on the bare floor. Less than an hour later, I was rudely woken up by a constable who told me that the SHO and the Deputy Superintendent of Police or DSP had come to take our statements.

One of them tapped his stick on my chest and said, "You are under suspicion like the rest." All the emotional turmoil I had gone through in the last twelve hours took its toll. "It is easy to suspect the innocent while the criminals..." The slap from the powerfully built SHO cut short my sentence. Let me finish with the others, I'll see you in the end. I spent a total of three days in this police station before the case was handed over to the Central Intelligence Agency or CIA, famous for "cracking" difficult cases. I was taken to the Saidu Sharif CIA police station.

I was handcuffed and then tied with a hook on the wall; my toes barely touched the floor. I had not slept for quite some time and would frequently doze off for a few minutes only to be awakened by the jerk from the hand cuffs.

Early in the morning the inspector of CIA came and said to me, "Make it easy for yourself and tell it all before we have to extract it out of you." Seeing a blank expression on my face (I think I had lost the power to speak), he started kicking and slapping me and after a couple of minutes, he was out of breath and left saying, "This is CIA, where even the hardened criminals break down." He ordered the other policemen to beat me till I confessed. These beatings continued for three days but I refused to confess to a crime I had not committed.

One of the ways of torture used by the police is hitting the soles of the feet with a stick. It does not leave any marks and is extremely painful. I do not know from where I got the strength to withstand this torture, but all this was nothing compared to what was next. When these beatings did not produce the desired results, they took me to the special interrogation room. My hands were tied behind my back and then with another rope my body was suspended from the hook in the ceiling upside down. My hands were below my head and all the body weight shifted to my shoulders and arms. The pain was most unbearable and I was crying out with pain. They would loosen the rope after every fifteen minutes and bring me down. The constables would then ask me why I was intent on getting my bones broken. Even if I was innocent I would not be spared the agony, unless I confessed, they said. After sometime, I lost consciousness and was carried back to the lock-up. The next day they took me before the magistrate. In Swat magistrates and session judges are called Qazis. The courts function in the same manner like the rest of the country and the judges have the same qualifications but the titles are changed. A magistrate is called *Ilaqa Qazi* and the Session Judge is *Zilla Qazi*. This trip was for recording my confessional statement. After my refusal, I was remanded back to the police station. I was produced before a doctor for the mandatory medical examination, but without even taking a look at me, he pronounced me fit for remand and did not find any marks of torture.

The same beatings and torture which had been going on for the last couple of days were repeated with even greater ferocity. The only moments of respite were when I was given breakfast (half a cup of tea), lunch, some boiled *daal* (lentil) and half *roti* (local bread) and dinner. These were given just to keep me alive. I tried to take as long as possible to eat as the momentary relief was nothing short of luxury. As my hands had been continuously tied above my head and due to the other torture, I started losing sensation in my arms and was unable to even grip the cup of tea. I was quite well built at the time of my arrest and had a muscular and athletic body as I did regular exercises and loved climbing mountains. Seeing the cup fall out of my hand, the constable who was guarding the lock-up brought another cup of tea and helped me drink it. After my experience in the police lock-up and in jail, I can safely say that the semi-literate and lower level policemen and jail wardens are far more sympathetic and kindhearted than their educated officers. Perhaps, their own poverty-related sufferings make them aware of the plight and feelings of their fellow humans.

Just when I had taken a few sips, the Inspector entered the lock-up and was furious with the constable saying in Pashto, “Is he the husband of your mother that you have put the cup of tea to his lips?”

“Sir, his hands are not functioning,” the constable replied. This worried the inspector a little and he ordered one of the constables to call the *malashi* (masseur) and left. The massager was one of the policemen who was earlier beating me. What paradox that the people responsible for giving me pain were now trying to relieve me of it. The constable said to me “Foolish boy do not act like Sanjay Dutt and Akshay Kumar (Indian film-stars). This is real life, so do as the *Sahib* (officer) says and spare yourself of the torture.” I did not have the energy or words to reply, but managed a broken and battered smile. Eleven years later, I find it rather offensive that he compared me with Sanjay Dutt, because I read in a press report that he broke down into tears after being sentenced to six years in prison.

During the initial days of my arrest I saw the father of the deceased a couple of times. He spent some time with the Inspector and when he came out of his room, he always gave me a ferocious look. The third time he came I called him saying “Uncle, please listen to me at least.” He came to me and said, “The Inspector is convinced that you have murdered my son”. I replied, “You know me since childhood. Why would I kill Zubair who was a dear friend and more like a brother?”

"My mind is paralyzed and I am just too confused to know what I should believe," he said and left. After having reflected innumerable times on his attitude especially in the solitude of the death cell, I do not blame him now, even though I was initially outraged. The shocking murder of his innocent young son had simply devastated him and it will surely haunt him for the rest of his life. After all, he loved his son just like my father loves me. The attitude of my father would not have been much different if the roles were reversed.

After I had spent 11 days in police custody, on the morning of 13 April 2000, he came to my cell again. By now, I had faced all the possible forms of mental and physical torture and humiliations. Every inch of my body ached with agony (pain does not accurately define what I was experiencing). My feet were swollen and it was impossible to even stand on my own.

He came to the lock-up and said in a most gentle voice, "Sohail, son, now I am convinced that you are innocent and if you were to make a confession before the Qazi today, where the Inspector is taking you, I will write a compromise deed and get you out. There is no other way out, believe me." I was 17 years old then and considered the brightest among my peers. I do not know why I fell for the trap perhaps because I was mentally exhausted and emotionally devastated and my body was all bruised and battered. This offer took all the fight out of me and I decided to confess the crime I did not commit. In jail, I was told that the night before taking an accused to court for confession, he is given drugged tea. I am not sure if that was the case with me. In the morning, I was taken under police escort to the court where I sat in a room while the Inspector went into the Qazi's court room. After an hour or so when I was being taken before the Qazi, the deceased's father met me outside the room and showed me some paper saying that they were the papers of the compromise deed, and everything was ready. I should do just as the Inspector had told me to do.

The Qazi just simply read out from the document in front of him and asked me if that was correct. After my "no" or "yes", he took my thumb impression and signature at the bottom of the document. Later I learnt that before recording the confession the magistrate should also ask the accused if he was tortured by the police and he should also be made aware that he is not bound to make a confession and that he will not be handed back to police custody. There are good magistrates who follow this procedure and there are others who do not. I was led out of the court room with two policemen helping me walk and the same procedure as before was repeated before the doctor, who found me fit with no torture symptoms or marks on me. I was taken to the big black gate of District Jail Swat, constructed by Wali-e-Sawat, who had also built the Jahanzeb College of which technically I was still a student.

CHAPTER 5

IN JAIL AND MY FIRST STEP TO STUDIES

"Do not wait to strike till the iron is hot; but make it hot by striking."

As I sat in the police mobile, my mind was numb and it slowly and gradually dawned on me as to what had happened and what lay in store for me. As soon as the threat of further torture had lifted, I was overcome with a sense of guilt for having shown weakness and confessed a crime I had not committed.

I had only a vague idea of what jail would be like. Maybe there would be prisoners breaking stones and a long mustached prisoner bossing the other, as in the Indian movies.

Entering the first gate of the jail, I was rather impressed by what I saw. There were small offices of the officers and everything was neat and clean. The policeman took off my handcuffs and handed me over to a jail warden. I was given a thorough body search, a couple of slaps and kicks, and pushed through yet another small gate into a big imposing black gate into the jail. This initial welcome of kicks and slaps did not have any effect whatsoever as I had grown accustomed to far worse treatment during the 11 days in police custody. Seven and half years back, it was a mandatory practice to beat up new inmates in jail to put fear of jail authorities into them, but things are much better now as beating and humiliation of prisoners for minor things or offences has almost entirely ceased.

Inside the black gate, I was rather surprised and again impressed by what I saw. The inner premises of the prison appeared somewhat similar to those of a Govt. High School I had seen. The walls were taller and instead of a door and windows there were iron bars and grills. There a numberdar (convicted prisoners who are assigned to help jail authorities and wear red caps and carry sticks) gave another thorough search and then helped me walk towards the juvenile barrack as my feet were swollen and I couldn't walk on my own. When I entered the barrack, the boys who were all roughly my age and some slightly older stood up to greet me. It is customary for inmates, especially among the juvenile prisoners, to greet fresh arrivals and make them comfortable. I inquired about my cousin and co-accused Rafiq, who had broken down earlier and made the confession a couple of days before me and was already in jail. I was taken to him and he was sitting with three other inmates roughly our own age; Usman, Alam and Haji Gul. They remained our friends and shared in cooking and preparation of food, cleaning the bunks and washing clothes.

Everybody shares what he has with other "Haandi Waals" (inmates occupying the same cell). As soon as we had settled down, Haji Gul announced lunch was ready. It was potatoes and green peas. I was most impressed by the food provided in jail. Later I was told it was not provided by jail authorities but was arranged and cooked by my "Haandi Waals".

My right hand was numb and I had to eat with the left hand and even though I had great difficulty in eating, it was one of the most delicious foods I had ever tasted. After the meal, Haji Gul massaged my shoulders and arms which relieved the pain a little. I was told that I should act like a man and try to walk on my own no matter how painful it was.

At four o'clock, the barracks were locked-up after counting the inmates in every barrack. In jail terminology it is called 'gintiband'. The barracks in jail are closed after Asr prayers and then reopened in the morning half-an-hour after Fajr prayers. In the daytime, they are again closed from 11 in the morning to 1 in the afternoon.

The other inmates had also suffered somewhat similar forms of torture but were taken aback when I told them what had happened to me, none of them had received such a savage treatment as I had and were therefore most sympathetic. After the evening meal, I lay down and a couple of other inmates including Haji Gul warmed some oil and massaged my shoulders, arms and feet. A piece of brick was warmed and then wrapped in a cloth and placed on various parts of the body which were black and blue with beatings. My feet after being thoroughly rubbed with warm oil were wrapped with bandages made of torn piece of cloth. As the barrack was over-crowded, I was given a space which was only two and half feet wide but it was still a luxury after the 11 nights in police look-up. Haji Gul brought a blanket and put it over me. Someone sent a glass of warm milk which soothed my nerves and I dozed off oblivious to everything. That first night for me, the jail was nothing short of a luxurious rest house or a five-star hotel.

The next day, a person came and gave me a small chit saying you have a visitor. Once a person is convicted, he has to perform different duties which are assigned to him according to his education, qualifications, strength and the build of his body. The strong and well-built are mostly made numberdars, a kind of social status regardless whether or not he has any particular skill like electrician, plumber, barber, etc. Those who can read and write properly are often made "munshis". A munshi is one who does the writing work. It was one such "munshi' who brought the slip to me. When I reached the "visitor's rooms", I saw my grandfather and younger uncle standing across the iron grills and meshing.

The first words my grandfather spoke were "Why have you committed the blunder of confessing a crime you did not commit?" He took one look at my face and said, "Don't worry, everything will turnout for the better, Inshallah (If Allah will sit)." We had a brief chat and I asked why papa had not come, and I was told that he will come in the next few days.

He did come after two days. Anguish was written all over his face and he looked exhausted. The expression on his face almost brought tears to my eyes and it was with some difficulty that I stopped myself from crying. We talked for less than half an hour and I could see that he was visibly devastated by what had happened. He had come to reassure and console me, but he himself needed it more than me. Before leaving he asked if there was anything he could bring for me. More than from my own need and desires, it was out of his love that I asked him to bring my first-year course and note books. This had the desired effect on him, as a faint smile appeared on his face and he left in slightly better spirits.

Gradually the pain in the body eased, but the emotional scars would take longer to heal. Soon I was becoming a part of the jail routine.

The structure of the barrack and cemented bunks varies from jail to jail. In Swat jail, the barrack was 38 ft. long by 14 ft. wide. At one end of the barrack, there was a small roofless toilet and a bathroom next to it, where one could bathe with a bucket. In front of each barrack, there was a small open space to take a walk. Swat jail being only a district jail and not a Central Jail did not have any proper walking ground.

Early in the morning, I would wake up and offer the Fajr prayers with the rest. Then the preparations for the breakfast would start. Cooking in jail is done on small stoves made from empty cooking oil and *ghee* (clarified butter) tins which are clayed from inside. Coals made from burnt-wood are used. Five kilogram packet of coal cost Rs. 35 at that time. It now costs Rs. 110. The jail authorities provide one third part of *Roti* — called "ticket" in jail terminology — for breakfast, and a small bucket of tea for every barrack. Normally we made our own tea and prepared breakfast. If we had a recent visitor from home the breakfast consisted of eggs and bread or we would simply warm the ticket and swallow it with the tea.

After breakfast we attended the compulsory religious classes where basic *Kalmas* (Islamic Oaths) and reading of Quran is taught by those convicted prisoners who have religious knowledge. Since I already knew these basic things, I just read one *Siparah* (Section of the Quran). After that I would busy myself with my course books. The books provided me with a mental escape and for once I started enjoying the studies which till then I had considered nothing more than a boring burden. After studying for three hours from 8 a.m. to 11 a.m., I would take a walk in the verandah and the very small court yard of the juvenile sector. At this time, my haandi waals would be busy in preparing the lunch. If none of us had a visit in the recent days, we would simply take the boiled daal (lentil) sent by the jail and fry it with tomatoes and onions and then have a hearty meal.

The memories of 11 days in police custody were still fresh so I rather enjoyed my early days in jail but I also suffered from bouts of depression when I would remember my family and how they would be suffering. It was to find an escape from such thoughts that I busied myself with my studies.

In the evenings, we would watch a black and white Russian TV. In the juvenile barrack, there was an old 'Baba' (term for an old man) prisoner to keep an eye on the juvenile prisoners. The one in our barrack was a lovely old fellow, Ahmed Jan

Baba, who would relate to me stories of his days in Bangladesh, where he was employed in a bank.

After the Maghrib prayers, we would have dinner and after the Isha prayers, I would again study till 11:00 p.m. My father and other family members would regularly come for visits and father would say only one thing, that I should forget everything and just concentrate on my studies. After a lot of efforts, he had managed to secure permission from the IG Prisons for me to take the exam in the examination hall. My father did not think it was proper to bring my mother to meet me in jail, but he told me that would bring her to meet me during my papers at the examination centre. When the exams started I experienced a different sort of emotional stress. A head constable and two policemen came to take me to the examination centre. The three of them were most friendly and encouraged, and praised me for my courage to have carried on studying even in jail. But the attitude of the superintendent of the examination hall was completely different. He gave me a glare filled with hate and said the most heart-breaking words, "So, a murderer has come from jail to take exams." I had to undergo a thorough body search. Having experienced much worse things I told him, "If I have knowledge in my head, I don't need to keep it in my pocket and socks." The boy sitting at the back of my chair was my college friend but he refused to shake my extended hand.

After I had taken the paper which went quite well despite my apprehensions, my father asked the head constable to allow me to have a meeting with my mother and family members in the Suzuki. The kind man that he was, the head constable readily assented. It was for the first time since my arrest that

I met my mother. She gave me a kiss on the forehead and all of a sudden broke down in tears. She would not let go of my handcuffed hands and kissed them. The exams also became a sort of family reunion as after every paper I had a chance of meeting my family, and most importantly, my mother.

CHAPTER 6

I PASS MY FACULTY EXAM, TRIAL CONTINUES

"It is not whether you get knocked down, it is whether you get up."

After the end of the exams, I started getting bored, and the jail started to take its toll mentally. Before and during the exams, I used to spend my time studying for exams, but now I felt a sort of vacuum in my life. I therefore asked my father to bring me some reading material. He would bring me different magazines and digests which also included children's magazines. It was not until after my conviction that I took interest in English books, novels and mostly digests. After reading them, I also felt an urge to write and started contributing short stories for these magazines and digests where one of my stories also won a prize.

The 30th of August 2001 was one of the happiest and most memorable days of my life. It was the day my first year FA (pre-grad) result was declared. The warden of our sector had become a friend of mine and he admired me for pursuing education even from jail. He himself was doing BA (graduation) as a private student, which is very rare for a jail warden. After the exams, he had taken my roll number and had told me that he would let me know the result when it was declared. That day he came literally running to my barrack (which too is quite rare for jail wardens except in cases of emergency) and said, "Sohail, give me a hundred rupee note and I'll tell you a wonderful news." I knew instantly that the results had been announced and that I had passed with at least reasonably good marks. I gave him the hundred rupees and he said that I had passed with good marks. I felt like I had conquered the world and embraced the warden. I also did a little dance.

The inmates of the barrack were well aware of my anticipation and anxiety about the results and seeing me so happy they all came and started congratulating me, especially my co-accused cousin Rafiq and other Haandi Waals embraced and hugged me. Although, I have passed many exams and even secured the 7th position in MA (Masters) in International Relations but I did not experience the same euphoric happiness again. That day I had felt myself to be on top of the world. I had proven that I was down but most certainly not out. I did not let my academic year be wasted and at least education wise I was at par with my class-fellows; but most importantly, despite my circumstances I had not let my father down. I put on my best clothes and sat anticipating with great joy the visit from my father. I started imagining how he would be brimming with happiness and beaming a big smile, which I had not seen in a long time. I imagined him in different poses with a box of *mithai* (sweetmeats) in hand. Perhaps he would make some special arrangement with the Superintendent or Deputy Superintendent and come inside the grilled and meshed visiting room to embrace me and give a kiss to me on the forehead. I waited for him all day long taking a walk in the courtyard of the sector. Just seeing the slip of paper containing my marks and roll number gave me great satisfaction. As time went by I started to wonder what was keeping him so long. I thought he must have decided to break the news first to my mother. I imagined him buying sweets on the way home; and my mother and grandmother would have raised their hands in a prayer to Allah on hearing the result; and how happily my grandfather would have taken a piece of sweet.

I waited for him well after the closing time of visits. Finally it hit me that he was not coming. What could have prevented him from coming? Did he consider me guilty like others and had not forgiven me for bringing a bad name? I walked back to the barrack dejectedly and lay on my bunk. I did not eat dinner. All night different ugly thoughts crossed my mind.

Next day Rafiq's brother came for a visit and brought a letter from my father. The letter read, "Sohail my son. There are certain strange moments in life when one is not sure to be either happy or sorrowful. After seeing the results I wanted to rush to you and congratulate you, but I could not bear the thought of congratulating you and breaking such great news to you from across the iron bars. I did not have the courage to break such wonderful news to you in such painful circumstances. Your mother is also most happy. She did cry a little both out of joy and sorrow. Salma and Laila (my sisters) are overjoyed and Daaji is the happiest of all. I have now recovered enough and will come along with Daaji tomorrow. Your mother will prepare food for the whole of your barrack. Sohail, keep it up my son. May Allah give you the strength and courage to bear the present misfortune."

In 2001, our case was put up for trial in the court of sessions judge, called *Zilla Qazi*, in Swat. He is a session judge and all the proceedings are the same like the rest of the country, only the court documents are in Urdu.

In order to strengthen the case, the police had also introduced a motive for murdering the deceased. Rafiq and I had allegedly committed theft in his house and then murdered him so as to hide the crime. The police had also claimed recovering certain stolen articles which included one set of binoculars, four *Shalwar Kameez* (the national dress made up of long shirt and loose fitting trousers), twelve under vests, twelve pairs of socks, etc. The CD player my father had gifted me on passing my matriculation exams was worth more than all these items put together. The most vital aspect of the case was our confessional statements. They were the most damning evidence and the whole prosecution case was based on that. The magistrate who had recorded our confessional statements stated on oath that he had observed all the legal formalities including giving me the assurance that I was not to be handed back to the police even if I refused to confess.

As I have stated earlier, the judge had not observed most of these formalities and handed me back to the police on two previous occasions when I had refused to record a confessional statement.

The day of the court appearance happens to be the most important day in the life of an under-trial prisoner. I keenly looked forward to the days of appearance in the court as I could breathe in the fresh air out of the lock-up. The days were rather like picnics as we helped ourselves to tea, biscuits, cakes, Pepsi and rice. All these things which were once an ordinary part of life now seemed like luxuries. It was also a lot easier to talk face-to-face with father unhindered by the bars of the lock-up and the iron meshing of the jail's visiting room. Our lawyer had assured us that it was only a matter of time and I would be free once the decision of the case was announced. This had greatly relaxed my father.

In the meantime, I was also preparing for the FA second year exams. Passing the first year exam with reasonably good marks had given me confidence and I knew despite all the difficulties, I would be able to pass the second year exams too. The second year exams started in May 2002. The policemen who came to take me to the examination hall were most friendly and gave me a lot of encouragement, and praised me a lot for showing courage and continuing my education even from jail. The superintendent of the examination hall this time around was also a friendly person and wished me well. I had secured more marks than most of my college mates who had rudely ignored me when I took the first year exam. I told the superintendent that I did not want to sit next to them so he put a separate seat for me at the front, away from them. As soon as the policemen took me in the examination hall, he told them to leave the hall saying "Take the handcuffs off, he is my responsibility".

Like the first year exams, the second year exams too provided an opportunity for a sort of family reunion. I met my mother again after one year. The policemen who brought me to the examination hall even allowed us to take pictures. My father and mother both seemed to be in better spirits. However when I took my last paper my mother clutched my hands tightly and started crying and asked my father, "Please don't let him go. Stop him please, don't let him go back to jail." This brought tears to the eyes of even the policemen who were anxious to get me back to the jail. My father assured her that not only will he take her to visit me in jail but also that 1 will be back home in a couple of months at the most as the trial of the case was near completion. He did bring her to meet me in the death cell.

The trial of our case completed with the argument of the lawyers on 22nd July 2002. The judge fixed the next day i.e. 23rd July for announcing the decision. I had a completely sleepless night. The next day I took a shower and put on my best clothes and took only a couple of sips of tea. I cannot describe in words the anxiety I was feeling. Our lawyer had repeatedly assured us that there was nothing to worry about as we were sure to get acquitted. His predictions and assurances as it turned out were as flawed as his capabilities as a lawyer. I kept on trying to reassure myself that I was sure to get acquitted as I had done no wrong.

CHAPTER 7

CONVICTED AND MOVED TO CENTRAL PRISON

"Being happy is not a matter of destiny.
It is a matter of options."

Before leaving the barrack, the fellow inmates wished me well and sent me off with prayers of acquittal. Haji Gul, my best friend, embraced me and told me not to forget bringing sweets after being acquitted.

I met my father in the lock-up was even more tense than me. He did not have the energy to say more than a few words. He ordered tea for us which remained untouched and he sat all alone on a bench away from the lock-up all lost in his own thoughts. My uncles, Rafiq's father, and his brother had also come. They were also under great stress.

It was after one o'clock that we were summoned to the courtroom. My father did not come with us. Rafiq's father, his brother and my younger uncle accompanied us. Upon entering the court room, the reader of the court took our thumb impression and then the judge announced with a straight face and expressionless voice, "The charges leveled against you are proved on the basis of your confessional statements, and recoveries made on your pointation thereby, I sentence you to death." By the time, I had entered the courtroom I was completely exhausted by the anxiety and lack of sleep. I did not feel anything, my mind had just gone blank and it was after I left the courtroom that the verdict slowly dawned on me. I felt as if the sky had fallen and as if a heavy stone had been placed on my head.

Once an accused is convicted the policemen try to rush him back to the jail to avoid any untoward incident. As we had been sentenced to death, the policemen were in a greater hurry. We were literally pushed into the prisoner's bus by the once friendly policemen.

As the bus was being reversed, I saw from the small opening in the bus, Rafiq's brother telling my father about the decision. I saw his head jerk towards the sky and as the bus left the court I saw he was still staring at the sky. That is to date my last vision of my father in the free air.

Once a prisoner is sentenced to death he is not kept with other prisoners in the barrack. The chief warden along with a guard of *numberdars* and other wardens took us to our cell and after giving us a thorough body search locked us in it along with an old prisoner. There is a rule in jail according to which only odd number of prisoners are kept in a cell that is one, three, or five. So we shared the cell with this fellow who was put there especially for us to make the number odd. I took an instant dislike to him. He had a long beard and the first words he spoke were like poison to me, "Boys, ask forgiveness from Allah for whatever great sin you have committed and for which you got this punishment at such a young age." Having himself been convicted for "whatever great sin" he had committed, it was impossible for him to imagine that a person could be sentenced to death even if he was not guilty.

As the news of our being sentenced to death spread, our friends and the other jail inmates rushed to our cell. They tried to calm and relax us, and I tried to put on a brave face and pretended as if nothing had happened. But all my internal feelings must have been apparent on my face. During my time on the death row (called *Phaansi Ghaat*), I have seen many people arrive after being sentenced to death and most of them try to pretend as if nothing has happened and all fail miserably. If nothing else, the new environment of a cell is enough to make one nervous.

The next day, my father, uncles and Rafiq's family members paid us a visit. The feeling of the meeting cannot be expressed in words. I desperately tried to put on a calm face and my father did not say much. After being sentenced to death, the prisoner is not allowed to go out of the confines of the small courtyard where the cells are located. So the visitors are brought to the cell and our small cell was crammed with family members. It would have been depressing for them to see us in this small an dirty cell.

On the 27th of July, three days after my conviction, the Chief

Warden came to our cell early in the morning and told us to get ready as we were being shifted to the Central Prison. We gathered what little possessions we had, and were not given a chance to say farewell to our friends; many of them did visit me in Haripur Central Prison after their release.

A head constable and three constables had come with a police mobile to shift us to Haripur jail. They were rather surprised to find that they were taking boys of our age and not some hardened criminals. This relaxed them and they were rather nice to us. When I stepped out of the jail gate to sit in the police mobile, I thought momentarily if these steps were the last steps I would ever take outside the premises of a jail.

As the police mobile van started its journey, I knew it would pass by one of my father's two filling stations. I desperately prayed that they would stop at it to get the tank filled with diesel and I would see my father and grandfather. But the mobile van simply rushed by the filling station and I did not see them. I did not know it then that my grandfather had stopped visiting the filling station ever since the time of my arrest.

While seeing the scenery from the mobile van, I kept on wondering if it would be the last time I was seeing the beautiful trees and fields and the small paths along these fields. This beautiful scenery, which once held no particular beauty and looked ordinary, seemed much more beautiful now. After travelling for about five hours, the mobile van stopped at a small roadside hotel. Judging from our age and appearance, the police were convinced that we were incapable of causing any trouble and had therefore decided to have breakfast. They also let us out of the mobile van to share the tea and *parathas* (local fried bread) with them. I glanced at the hotel's signboard; which read, 'Insaf Hotel, Attock' (Justice Hotel).

Despite everything I did try to enjoy the breakfast, as it was the first I was taking in the open air sitting on a proper cot after two years and I thought, possibly the last. The owner of the hotel was an acquaintance of the driver of the police mobile and learning that we were condemned prisoners, refused to charge any money. I have often daydreamed that when I am released, on the way home we'll stop at the same hotel for lunch, and I would introduce myself to the owner.

It was some minutes past noon, when the mobile van stopped in front of a big gate of an imposing building of the Central Prison Haripur. I checked the time on the watch my father had gifted me for passing my first year exams.

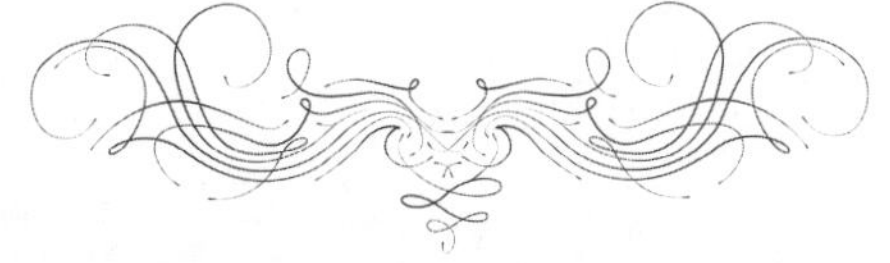

CHAPTER 8

I APPEAR IN BACHELORS' EXAM FROM DEATH ROW

"Toughness is in the soul and spirit, not in muscle."

The death row (sector of the jail where the cells of prisoners condemned to death are located) is a jail within the Jail. After our arrival in Haripur Central Prison, the Chief Warden and his guard of convicted prisoners (called *numberdar*) escorted us to the death row. As we entered through the wooden door of the sector, I saw a long row of steel bars on my right side and in front of them was a verandah. Beyond the verandah, there was a small dusty ground in the middle of which stood an old banyan tree. We were locked in Cell no. 17 with Gul Muhammad who looked only slightly older than us. He stood up to greet us and tried to make us feel comfortable. He had been in the death cell for the last four years and was about 22 years old.

On our first meeting, Gul Muhammad told us about life on death row. The cells remain locked for 22 hours of the day.

They are opened twice for one hour each: once in the morning and once in the evening to let the inmates have a walk. The inmates on the death row are not allowed to go beyond the confines of the sector. They take a walk in the small ground with handcuffs on both hands. He advised me not to have too much contact with the other inmates as they were not only older than us, but most of them were hardened criminals and sometimes quite desperate and frustrated.

From then on, I lost track of time and like the rest of the inmates my life revolved around waiting for the time of our walk.

The cell of a prisoner condemned to death is 12 ft. (length) by 8 ft. (width). The front part, about 6½ ft. long, forms the living area, which the three of us shared. The back portion is divided into two parts, one part has a commode and a bucket of water. It serves as the toilet and the bathroom. It is separated from the rest of the cell by a cloth curtain. The other part serves as a kitchen. Gul Muhammad was too poor to do his own cooking and ate the food provided by jail, with our arrival he assumed the responsibilities of a cook while I and Rafiq would wash the clothes and clean the cell. When Gul Muhammad was very young, his parents had divorced and both his father and mother had remarried. None of them ever came for a visit.

After we had spent a week in Haripur Prison, Papa came for a visit along with mother and Rafiq's brother. They sat on an old bedsheet across the three feet wide gate of the cell. Mother started crying and stopped only when Papa told her not to make life more difficult for me. I could not bear to see my mother sitting on the floor. I wanted to tell her not to visit again but did not have the heart to do so. After mother had calmed down a little, Papa told me that the appeal had been filed in the Peshawar High Court. I told him I wanted to do BA in Political Science and Law as I wanted to be a lawyer if I was acquitted. My mother and father both replied at once that I was sure to be acquitted. I asked my father to bring a black and white television for me as prisoners on the death row were allowed to keep their own televisions in Haripur Prison. Smuggled Chinese color televisions had not yet flooded the market and it was rare for a prisoner to have even a black and white television; having a color television was almost unheard of.

My father left saying he would come again after a month or so. He came sooner than that; in fact he came the very next Thursday. Prisoners in the death cell are allowed visits on Thursdays and Mondays only. Out of nowhere, he stood at the door of the cell and I stood up with a jerk as I saw his smiling face across the door. I had passed the FA exams in first division and was 9th amongst my college fellows. Along with the BA (Part I) course books, he gifted me a large radio and a color television. The inmates on the death row are as conscious of status symbol as the rest of the society. Six years ago, owning a color television on the death row was like owning a brand new sports car in real life. My prestige enhanced a great deal.

I devoted my time less to my studies and more to listening to the radio and watching television. After almost three years in the lock-up, even the news and current affairs programs seemed very interesting.

After a couple of months, I started feeling really depressed and dejected. I felt bored with television and lost interest in Urdu magazines, especially the children's digests which Papa had brought. I, then, turned towards my course books. And, this gave me the feeling of doing something positive and not wasting my time even in the death cell. I was, however, having difficulty in understanding some of the chapters of Law and Political Science, and English was not too easy either. When I learnt that there was a very educated man in jail, whose name was Mr. lqbal, I sent a short letter to him stating that I had already passed FA from jail and was looking to pursue further education. He came after seeking permission from the chief warden. He was about 55 years old and had worked in UNO. He gave me great encouragement and offered to help out with the studies. Prisoners on the death row are kept isolated from other prisoners, and Mr. Iqbal was allowed to visit me only once or twice every week.

The superintendent makes a visit (called 'parade') of the whole jail twice every month and inquires from the prisoners about their problems. On the next parade, I asked the superintendent to allow Mr. lqbal to teach me daily. I told him I had already done my FA from Swat prison. The superintendent was most impressed and gave a lot of encouragement and promised to facilitate me in every way possible. Mr. lqbal taught and helped me with English, Political Science and Law. He also introduced me to the world of English books. He gave me Nelson Mandela's *Long Walk to Freedom* to read. I found it hard to understand. I was very weak in English, so I would underline the sentences I did not understand and ask their meaning from him the next day. I still have that book and a great part of it is underlined with Urdu meanings written with pencil. Just when I had almost completed the course with him, he got released on bail. Even after his release, he remained a regular visitor till he got a job abroad.

Shortly after Mr. lqbal had departed, I learnt that a *Gora* (Caucasian) as a prisoner had come to jail. Professor Stuart — convicted for trying to smuggle heroin from Peshawar airport — was my new teacher. The only subject he could and did teach me was English. He understood very little of Urdu and we conversed in English. He would then correct the mistakes. It was through Stuart that I read my first English novel Sidney Sheldon's *Rage of Angels*. I became addicted to English novels and on the next visit, I asked my father to bring me English novels.

The BA (Part I) examinations were held in June 2003. The prisoners confined in the death row are not allowed even beyond the confines of the sector. For the first time (at least in Haripur Prison), an examiner was coming to the death row. (How my father managed to secure the permission from university and other authorities is a different story.)

The anxiety of exams replaced the fear of life and death. The hype of exams in the distressed atmosphere of the death cell made me actually fearful of the exams. Thankfully, the first paper was compulsory English for which I was well prepared. I sat ready for the paper half-an-hour before the scheduled time of 9:00 a.m. as mentioned in the university date-sheet but with every passing minute I felt more tense. When the examiner did not come even fifteen minutes after the starting time, I was almost convinced that the exam would not be held at all. I was sitting dejectedly in the cell when the examiner arrived. Being unaware of the rigid procedures of jail, he came at exactly nine but had to wait. He was let in after a thorough search and was accompanied by a warden. He felt visibly humiliated. As he handed me the paper, he told me that he was not at fault for being late and will not allow me any extra time. We sat on a mat spread under the Banyan tree. I placed the answer sheet on my lap and started writing. The paper was rather easy and I found no major difficulty in attempting it. A student taking exam from the death cell of the jail was something new and unique in the short history of the newly established Hazara University. Half way through the paper, two inspectors deputed to check the examination hall came for a surprise check. I was taking the paper with my back to the door of the sector. I was fully engrossed in doing the paper and did not notice them coming. One of them was himself an English professor and was rather impressed by my paper. They left after asking a couple of questions about my education from jail and how I had prepared for the exams. The next papers were taken by different examiners and each of them swore to never visit the jail again for conducting an examination.

CHAPTER 9

I PASS MY BACHELORS' DEGREE

"The game of life is not so much playing a good hand, but playing a bad hand well."

After the end of exams, I found an even greater pleasure in reading the novels. I sent a letter to the two Jail libraries (one was established in the British era and had some rare books, some of them printed in late 1800s and the other in the juvenile sector established by an NGO) requesting them to send me any interesting books of their choice. The two librarians came with copies of lists of books in their library. They had come personally out of curiosity to meet the first person to have taken the BA exam from the death cell. The books which I read included, *Shahabnama*, which I found really interesting and impressive then, but do not like it as much now. I also read Mumtaz Mufti's *Alipur ka Ally*, Ibn-e-Insha's most humorous books, Sibt-e-Hassan's books, British History, Russian History, History of Islam, Indo-Pak History and books about General

Knowledge. I also read Charles Dickens' *Oliver Twist* and *Great Expectations*, etc. It was when I was reading all those books and novels, that I dreamed of myself becoming a writer one day.

Because I was so young and devoted so much time to reading, the wardens were much impressed and liked me a lot. I had requested one of them, Shahnawaz, who also belonged to Swat to let me know when the result was declared. On 13th August 2003, Shahnawaz told me that the result had been announced and waved the local newspaper which contained the result (also known as 'the Gazette') demanding three hundred rupees. Market price of the local newspaper was three rupees, but it is not the most expensive newspaper I have ever bought. Even though I had passed only in the second division yet merely passing the exam was good enough for me. I gave him my father's phone number to tell him the news. The description of my next meeting with father would need a whole episode. The scene of a father and mother congratulating their son for passing an exam from the death cell cannot be described in words.

The day of 16th August 2003 was the saddest and most sorrowful day of my life in the death cell. Gul Muhammad was taken to Tameergarah prison (an area near Swat) for execution — to be hanged by the neck till death. The land on which Haripur prison is constructed was leased to the British by a woman on the condition that no hangings will take place here and so it does not have the facility of gallows. Prisoners whose appeals and mercy petition to the President are rejected are taken to prisons in their native areas for execution. The chief warden allowed us to see him off from the wooden door of the sector. I vividly remember him leaving the sector taking short steps, almost dragging his feet. I remember the wave of his hand and the look on his face with tears streaming down his cheeks. May Allah Almighty bless his pure soul, he was a true friend. Even after more than four years, tears come to my eyes when I remember the last months of his life he spent with us and the scene of our last meeting.

Since there was no other prisoner of our age on the death row, Rafiq and I were put in separate cells. According to jail rules, only an odd number of prisoners may occupy a cell i.e. either one or three. Many cells were empty at that time, I saw the cells fill up during five and half years, most of them being shared by three inmates. Moving to separate cells posed some small problems like, who would keep the television. I had found books to be more interesting so I left the television with Rafiq and moved into Cell no. 16 along with my radio and my books. I spent a sleepless night. I was feeling extremely sad for Gul Muhammad and was very uncomfortable being all alone in the cell. The next day I asked the head warden who allowed me to spend the day with Rafiq and was locked back in my cell in the evening.

As I had difficulty in sleeping, I developed the habit of reading well past midnight. While reading the books, my mind took an escape from the harsh realities and I found myself amongst the characters and situations mentioned in the books. I also tried to study the BA (Part II) course books, but I found English Jurisprudence (Law) and Constitutions of Pakistan, China, UK and USA really difficult to understand. In December 2003, Stuart got released but before leaving he had acquainted me with another white South African, Professor Les (also convicted for trying to smuggle heroin) who was in his late forties and had tattoos on his ankles and around the wrists. Even though I continued to improve my English, I was yet, unable to understand most of the law and political science course. Then Allah Almighty gave me a wonderful teacher. A real professor. He was a retired Major of the Armed Forces. He had a Master's degree in Strategic Studies and taught me law and the constitutions. If not for him, I would have never passed the exam. He brought his English newspaper with him and after explaining to me the background and significance of the main news he would leave the newspaper with me to read it, afterwards telling me to especially read the opinion columns. I finished the course with him twice. The first time he explained in broad terms all the topics of law and political science and the second time he read each and every line of the two prescribed course books. He explained each and every sentence written in those books to me.

He also introduced me to different kinds of books; especially non-fiction. He got released in April 2004 two months before the exam, but by then I was already quite well prepared.

This time in addition to the studies, I made a different sort of preparation. I had my hair cut and combed carefully before the start of the papers, put on white clothes and tried to look my best. I knew the examiners this time would be coming to meet with great curiosity the person who had passed BA (Part I) from the death cell. Most of them were rather amazed to find that the death cell was after all not a dark deep underground dungeon. In fact, it resembled a small hostel room with a color television.

They had to be told that, "one spent twenty two hours in this room." On the special directions of the superintendent, no great delays occurred this time and the papers started almost on time. The examiners however, had the harassed look that one has if surrounded by desperate criminals.

When the result was declared, I had passed again only in second division, but I had firm conviction that I'll achieve the ultimate, and do my Masters in International Relations (IR). In addition to the celebration, something took place which is unheard of in any jail in the whole world. The superintendent sent a box of sweets to a prisoner in the death cell. I gave the phone number of my father to the warden and asked him to tell my father the news. I offered prayers of *Shukraana* (Thanks to Allah Almighty) and for the next few days I forgot, I was on the death row.

CHAPTER 10

I PASS MY MASTERS' IN INTERNATIONAL RELATIONS

"Happy are those who dream dreams and are paying the price to make them come true."

After having passed BA, I decided to do a Masters in International Relations and asked my father to bring me the course books. I could have done Masters in Political Science or History but by then I had developed a certain interest in International and Current Affairs. I had started getting the English newspaper daily. Even though my father brought the books on the next visit, he asked me to choose a different subject. He had been told that it was almost impossible for me to pass the International Relations papers from jail without attending a university. I was confident and having already passed BA, I had faith in my ability and the will to work hard. More than anything else, I wanted to do my Masters in IR for the sake of knowledge. It did not matter to me if I passed or failed.

I started preparing for the exams with the aid of an atlas. If I wanted to do a Masters' Degree in International Relations, it was of course necessary to know the exact locations of the important countries first. I also had an English newspaper delivered to my cell daily. Since I had no one who could help me, I wrote letters to the Head of International Relations Department of Hazara University and to Dr. Adnan Sarwar Khan, the Head of International Relations Department of Peshawar University whom I had seen in the current affairs programs on television. They sent me encouraging letters giving tips for the preparation of exams and also sent notes.

My cousin and co-accused, Rafiq had also re-started his academic career. My passing BA Part I exams had encouraged him, and after having passed FA, he was now preparing for BA exams, while I was preparing for MA exams.

By reading newspapers and watching current affairs programs on my black-and-white television (the color television was in Rafiq's cell), I had become quite well aware of international events, but studying the actual course books presented a different problem. I had difficulty in understanding most of the topics not related to the international affairs. The only teacher I had was Les, the South African, who helped improve my English but his knowledge of international relations was even less than mine.

Rafiq too was preparing for his BA exams. He had chosen Law

and International Relations. His exams were to be held in June 2005, and mine in August 2005. His preparation for the exams posed certain problem as he did all the main chores, including the cumbersome process of cooking, which took up the major part of a prisoner's time. It takes skill and at least ten minutes to merely light the stove. Even though the stove itself is very small and made from five liter empty oil tins, it would fill the small cell with smoke and made it hot like an oven during the summers. It was, I think, the main reason for making Rafiq sick and having him undergo treatment. Thanks to Almighty Allah, he got fully cured after taking the medicines. I was a terrible cook. In fact, I had great difficulty in peeling and cutting the vegetables with the sharpened handle of the tea spoon, which Rafiq of course, managed effortlessly. Keeping knives in the cell, however small, is a great offence; and even tea spoons made from steel are confiscated in the very frequent 'search operations'. Rafiq is convinced that one day he will own a chain of five star hotels and I will just be a poor professor unable to afford a lunch in one of his hotels.

As Rafiq's exams approached, we ate nothing but fried eggs three times a day for weeks and, sometimes, we also ate daal (lentil) from the jail mess just to change the taste. I used to wait for the visit from Papa more anxiously than ever, as on every visit he brought with him home-cooked rice — *Biryani* (spiced rice with meat), *Kabli Pulao* (steamed rice with raisins, carrot and lamb) — and other really exotic foods like *Shaami Kebabs* (fried minced meat patties) and fried fish.

When my exams started, I was not only under-prepared, but my handwriting speed was also too slow and I could not attempt the required five questions even in a single paper. When the exam ended I had no illusion what the result would be but I felt a satisfaction for at least having taken the exams. The result was slightly better than my expectations. I had managed to pass all the papers but failed to secure the required aggregate of fifty percent marks, which meant instead of taking the whole exam again I could choose two papers of my own choice and secure enough marks in them to get the aggregate fifty percent.

On the visit after the result was announced, I told Papa about the result. He encouraged me and told me not to worry. He had also brought my younger brother, Shiraz with him. He is five years younger than me and was a student of fifth class when I was arrested. Papa had brought him only three or four times during the last six years. Papa thought bringing him to jail would have a negative effect on him. Papa had brought him to meet me as he had now grown up. He was 17 years old. I was surprised to meet him after more than a year. With the grace of Almighty Allah, he had grown up very quickly and looked taller than me. "Don't worry bhai jan, I am sure you will pass with good marks next time," he said. Advice and encouragement coming from him sounded strange, especially after the long gaps and meeting him only occasionally in between. I still had his image as a child for whom I brought samosas, pakoras, chips, sweets and chocolates; all those things which I myself now longed for.

Shortly after the result was declared I met Aamir Ali Shah, who was an under-trial prisoner. He was a law graduate undergoing apprenticeship when he got arrested. He was preparing for the CSS exams and hence, helped me a great deal in my preparation. He was a daily visitor till his acquittal and gave me valuable advice, about preparing for the exams and how I should attempt the papers. On his advice, I copied word for word the important topics in my own handwriting and then tried to rewrite them in my own words, this also helped a great deal in improving my hand writing speed. In addition to studying from course books and notes, I copied important articles about international issues and events from the newspapers. I also paid great attention to current affairs program on television and on Aamir Ali Shah's advice, I also listened to *BBC* and *VOA* on the radio. Listening to the 8 p.m. evening Urdu bulletin of *BBC*, he told me was a must. I also read the quarterly *Strategic Studies* journal, sent free by the Institute of Strategic Studies Islamabad. They had returned the Rs. 200 worth of postal tickets, saying they would be ashamed if they accepted the subscription fee sent from a death cell. The *FRIENDS* organization also sent its quarterly journal, books published by their organization and clippings of important news and articles, which proved most helpful. When the exams started, I was well prepared and fully focused, unlike the previous exams. I did not even bother to change the clothes I had slept in. I had no difficulty whatsoever in either the two MA (Part I) papers or the MA final papers. My writing speed was also much improved and for the first time in my life, I needed extra sheets in addition to the main answer notebook.

After the end of exams, I felt both strangely exhausted and mentally relaxed at the same time as if I had climbed to the top of a mountain.

But the job was only half done. The viva voce was to be

conducted within a couple of weeks. I was not even sure if the university would send a professor to conduct the oral examination. I was notified that a professor sahib would come for the exam on 4th November 2006. I felt a strange joy as after five years I would be meeting someone else other than the inmates, prison staff and visitors, who were almost always relatives or friends. I did not have any conversation with the examiners who came to give me my papers, as I did not have time, and they sat quietly just keeping a close watch. I felt really nervous and tried to prepare the answer for any questions he might ask. I started to imagine what he would look like. The Professor when he came looked strongly similar to what he had looked in my imagination. He was tall, thin, with graying hair and even wore glasses. He said since I had taken the exams in difficult circumstances I myself should choose a topic from which he should ask the questions. Without any hesitation I replied, "Current Affairs." As I answered his question, he asked questions related to other topics as well. The learned Professor asked me how even from the death cell I had gained such knowledge, because I had answered many questions which most of his regular students could not have. When I told him about my sources of information and the teachers, he parted after offering prayers for my acquittal saying the standard of education and teaching was at par if not better then the Hazara University.

I had never before slept as soundly as I did in those few days after the exams. I felt myself to be like the shepherd in *The Alchemist*, a Paulo Coelho novel, when he found the secret to the treasure, after being all battered and bruised.

As my papers and viva voce had gone very well, I was waiting anxiously for the result. I had started getting the local newspaper daily which always printed the BA and MA results. It was 24th February 2007, when the news was announced on its front page that MA results had been declared. I felt so anxious and nervous I gave the newspaper to Rafiq to check the result because my hands were shaking. After checking the result Rafiq, gave me a strange look and my heart skipped a beat. Then he embraced me. Not only had I passed but also only six other roll numbers had more marks than mine. Rafiq told me he wanted to play a joke on me by lying that I had failed, but the expression on my face had changed his mind. He thought I would have had a heart attack.

CHAPTER 11

DEATH SENTENCE COMMUTED TO LIFE

"If I act with goodness, I will receive goodness. If I act with evil I will get evil."

After the result was declared, Papa, Shiraz and mother came to congratulate me. All of them looked extremely happy. Papa and mother kissed me on the forehead through the small gap in the bars of the gate of the cell. Shiraz shook my hands so strongly that it hurt my fingers. Papa looked very happy saying I had made him proud, but there was a worried sort of look appeared on his face every now and then. I thought he must be feeling sad to be congratulating me across the gate of a death cell. I found out the real reason a couple of weeks later! One of the inmates gave me an Urdu newspaper *Jang*, which stated "arguments heard and the decision reserved to be announced at a later date in the appeals filed by two prisoners M. Rafiq and Sohail Fida, who had been sentenced to death by Zilla Qazi, Swat."

After our conviction, an appeal had been filed before the Peshawar High Court in August 2002, but as we had also been charged with theft under the Hudood Ordinance, the Honorable Court had dismissed the appeal to be filed before the Federal Shariat Court. After a year or so of filing of the appeal, I do not remember exactly how many Honorable Judges (one or two) retired. Cases involving murder can only be heard by a full bench and since the bench was not complete our case could not be put up for hearing.

When I was waiting for the result, I remember hearing on the television news channels and reading in the newspaper about the appointment of two Honorable Judges in the Federal Shariat court. At that time, I had other things on my mind. I thought due to the backlog of cases there was no chance of our appeal being heard any time in the near future. The news of the decision of our case being reserved came as a really big shock. I had never felt before the way I was feeling after hearing the news. My mind sort of went numb and I started thinking about my fate. Will I get acquitted and go back to my family and home or will I be "hanged till death"? If you grant a wish to any prisoner except acquittal, his reply would be that he wants to die in any manner other than being hanged, as it really is the most humiliating and inhuman form of death. Every day that I waited for the decision of the case, I wondered if my father would have the heart to tell me personally if the death sentence was upheld. My mind had received such a shock that I started imagining bizarre scenes, such as "Sohail Fida MA (IR)" would be written on my tombstone. I had even started to think about what my last wish would be. It was just the shock that made me think such bizarre and often stupid thoughts. Rafiq was much more composed and in a better frame of mind. I thought perhaps the other inmates were right when they said reading and studying too much would ultimately make me insane. Rafiq advised me to start praying regularly and seek the blessings of Almighty Allah. Turning towards the Almighty relieved the tension and I found peace. I also started to see things from a different perspective. I thanked Almighty Allah for his countless blessings which had enabled me to complete my education and had provided me with the means to do so even in the death cell which was thought to be a Godforsaken place — a deep dark dungeon. I saw how miserable the lives of many of the other inmates were. Many of whose families had been deprived of their sole bread earners and also how poverty stricken they were. Some had to sell everything to meet the different expenses, including fees of the lawyers. Some could not afford their own lawyers. Those who cannot afford are provided "Pauper's counsels" by the court because they had nothing to sell. Many gave up everything they owned for a compromise, but they at least got a chance to live again. There were others who were willing to offer money not just in millions but in tens of millions for compromise, but their lives were not spared. On at least two occasions, the unfortunate prisoners had offered over ten million rupees, but a compromise could not be affected and so they had to face death. On the other hand, I had seen people acquitted or their sentence commuted to life imprisonment even if they couldn't afford a lawyer. Some, I heard after having been taken for the final execution, were forgiven at the last minute for the sake of Allah by the relatives of the deceased. The most heartbreaking stories were when the relatives of the deceased forgave the prisoner when the sister, mother, or daughter of the prisoner threw her *dupatta* (stole) or *chaddar* (shawl) on the feet of the male having the authority to effect a compromise.

I started to thank Allah, for having provided me with a loving and caring family who kept faith and believed in me. I also thanked Him, for providing me excellent teachers even in the death cell other than those about whom I have mentioned here, there were some with whom I had only a brief contact. They included a retired Major Sahib, an old senior advocate of High Court, and a prisoner on the death row who taught me the art of Urdu writing. I started feeling very close to Allah. I felt a euphoric closeness to Him, Who alone has the power to make possible what may seem impossible. It wasn't difficult for Him to provide me with knowledge in the death cell.

I was amazed when I thought about the teacher who had appeared almost suddenly and disappeared also as quickly when I needed the help most. It all could not have been a series of coincidences. Thinking about Sohaila and her grave, which is mentioned earlier, I wondered if I could ever see her again in a dream; but despite my prayers I did not. May be she was just one of my teachers who had left after teaching me that nothing is impossible, it is just that there are some truths which may seem unbelievable.

Reading the 'Letters to the Editor' page of an English newspaper, I, one day, had the idea of writing a letter to the editor, narrating the details of my story and educational achievements. I also wanted to share with the readers that if one had the will, even the most difficult task becomes achievable. My story was also printed in some main Urdu dailies, including a full feature with the picture of my DMC. I got an excellent response from all different sections of society especially from jails. A couple of them stated that, they were inspired by my story, and decided to pursue further education. One kind man sent a money order of Rs. 200 along with a letter asking me to buy *mithai* for myself. He expressed his embarrassment at being unable to send me more money. Even, people from India responded to letters in the English newspaper. While some wrote directly to me, others got their letters published in other newspapers. I was still busy reading the books sent by a few of the readers of my story and responses to letters, when Federal Shariat court went on vacation.

I was now, at least for a couple of months fully free of the daily routine of waiting for the decision, even though I was far less anxious, but the wait was still there. One day I read about a book, *Memoirs and Reflections of a Pakistani Diplomat* by Sultan M. Khan in the 'Books & Authors' page of the *Daily Dawn*. I wrote a letter in Urdu to its publisher and, counting on their generosity, tried to persuade them to send me the book. I got the book along with a really encouraging letter from Mr. Muhammad Ali Khan, then General Manager of the publishing company with the offer that he would send me another wonderful book, if I sent him a summary of this book. The book was most interesting as it detailed the background occurrence of many events I had read about in MA (International Relations). I was greedy for another book and also touched by his interest, so I wrote a long letter to him, which included a small summary of the book. I did not know that this letter would lead me to the fulfillment of the ultimate dream of me getting the story of my life printed as written by me.

Mr. Muhammad Ali Khan was of course, like everybody else, unaware of the quality of teaching at Haripur Central University and was rather shocked by my reply. He got so excited that he asked my permission (I do not understand why he needed it) to get it printed in the 'Books & Authors' of the *Sunday Dawn* newspaper. After granting permission, I started waiting for its publication, but before this could happen, I received on 27th July 2007 a literally breathtaking news. One of the prisoners assigned to perform the duties of carrying messages (often written on small papers) came to our cell and called me. I thought he had brought the mail but what he told shocked me and I stood breathless for a while. The Federal Shariat court had converted our death sentence to life imprisonment i.e. 25 years of imprisonment. Papa had phoned the jail authorities and requested them to convey the news to me. Because all the jail officers were acquainted with me, they did this as a favor to me. Such news is not conveyed to the prisoners unless the source is official. Commutation of life imprisonment did not mean I was to be let out of the cell immediately. First, the order would be sent to Zilla Qazi (session judge) Swat, who would then pass it to District Jail Swat and from there to Haripur prison. It took almost a month before we were finally let out of the cell. I do not think any other prisoner, after being commuted to life imprisonment and not acquitted, will ever spend a happier month and enjoy it as much. I not only had a new lease of life but the letters published in *Dawn*, evoked an overwhelming response. I received letters daily from professors, doctors, engineers, students, authors, retired army officers, lawyers, human rights organizations, serving and retired civil servants, even from as far as the US. Ambassador Sultan M. Khan wrote a most kind and praiseworthy letter.

My cell was flooded with boxes full of books on every possible topic ranging from *Exploits of Gama Pehlvan* — it's such pity I can't read it as it is written in Punjabi, to *101 Most Influential People who Never Lived* — about imaginary characters that did not exist but still made a difference. The readers, of course, were not aware of the commutation of my death sentence to life imprisonment and some even thought, I was quite near to the death sentence date. I had to write responses to such a large number of letters that my fingers ached. However, one thing was sure, my hand writing speed would be extremely fast by the time I was to appear for my MA (History) exams, which were not far away.

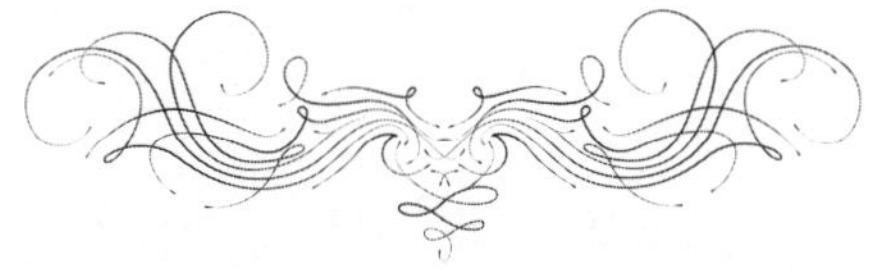

My road was flooded with boxes full of books on every possible form, ranging from [illegible] to [illegible] suddenly I [illegible] read it as it is written in [illegible] by [illegible] [illegible] abound [illegible] many characters that did not exist but still made a difference. The [illegible] of course, were not aware of the [illegible] of my death [illegible] to [illegible] amusement, and some even thought I was quite [illegible] the [illegible] that I had to write [illegible] to [illegible] a large number of letters that [illegible]. The [illegible] language [illegible] my hand writing speed would be [illegible] by the time I was [illegible] which was not far away.

CHAPTER 12

BACK IN THE BARRACK

"Rock bottom is good solid ground. A dead end is just the place to turn around."

When father came for 'the visit', as I call it, all that had occurred in the last seven-and-half years was summed up in a single dialogue. As the visiting time came to an end, I couldn't resist saying, "Papa you have suffered greatly."

"Yes Sohail, and that's the only thing I ever wanted to hear from you. All my sufferings have been relieved now that you have said it." As he was leaving, I saw — after almost seven and half — years a genuine smile on his face. I had started thinking what my fate would be when I was 17 years old and finally stopped thinking about it when I had done Masters' at the age of 24. I had come to the death row empty-handed, a student of FA (my result had not been declared), I would be walking again through that wooden door of the sector with a Master's degree and going to find out what the real jail was all about. I had spent these five and half years not in a death cell, but in a hostel room cut off from the world.

Waiting for the arrival of documents, I spent my last days in the death cell with mixture of happiness, excitement and slight apprehension. I was, of course, overjoyed at getting a new lease of life, but I also wondered if I would be able to readjust to life in the barrack. The thought of moving back to the life in barrack after spending more than five years in the relative solitude of the death cell made me nervous and I felt more self-conscious. I would not be alone in a small room (especially at night), but share a barrack with other inmates. I was also excited by the prospects of the new life where I would be able to take a walk at most times of the day, whenever I liked and without handcuffs. It was 23rd of August 2007, when after a lapse of more than five years, I set foot outside the wooden door of the sector and what a wonderful feeling that was. I was first taken to the office where all the paper work regarding prisoners is done. I walked for around five minutes on the paved path, which I had walked on five years ago on my arrival in Haripur Prison. I noticed the trees and the beautiful flowers along the path and wondered how I could have missed noticing them the first time. The walk to and back from the offices seemed like a walk in the Shalimar Gardens (Historical Moghal Gardens in Lahore), which I remembered having visited, in another life. I had visited the Shalimar Gardens when I was just an innocent boy, during one of our winter trips with my family. I was then not a convicted thief, brutal murderer, or an outcast thrown to rot in jail.

That first night, I spent in the barrack seemed as if I was

on a different planet. I felt like an animal back in the jungle after having spent most of his life in a cage. The inmates were friendly and welcoming, and were well-aware of our educational qualifications attained from the most dreaded place in jail. They tried to strike up a conversation but I was just too confused to understand what they were saying. I remembered my first night in Swat Prison, where after 11 days I had found the jail to be rather luxurious and comfortable and had gone to sleep immediately. As the inmates went to sleep, the televisions and radios were turned off at the cutoff time of 10:00 p.m. and the night became quiet. I started to remember my first nights in the death cell. I would then wonder about the fate of those who had lived in the cells before me and was fearful of my own fate. I remembered my dreams, which I dreamt with open eyes. With the passage of time, my dreams had also changed with the exams I passed. From driving the latest model car to becoming the first prisoner to do Ph.D. and getting my name in the Guinness Book, writer of a bestselling book and an expert on International Affairs, a movie made on the life of a genius locked in the death cell, etc. I also dreamt of what I am doing now, writing the story of my life.

I realized as I breathed in the cool and refreshingly free air of the barrack that I had spent five years actually in a grave. I thanked Almighty Allah for providing me with light of knowledge even there. I started to feel like a rescued person, who had been shipwrecked on an island. Finally, I went to sleep praying the dream may not turn into a nightmare this time.

MA (History) exams were just a couple of weeks away. Studying while sitting under the trees on the ground of the sector was a pleasure in itself. My interest in History as a subject had been aroused ever since I read Sibt-e-Hassan's *Maazi kay Mazaar*, *Naveed-e-Fikar* and *Pakistan main Tehzeeb ka Irtiqa*. His writings had shaken my religious beliefs a little for sometime, but the fear of the Almighty Allah and the desperate need for His help in the death cell had in the end proved more powerful than some of his views. I wonder what his views would be about Sohaila's grave — just a passing thought? After five years, I felt strange taking the exams sitting on a chair. I was also not alone. There were four or five other prisoners as well, taking MA Islamic Studies exams. I hoped the professors would agree with my version of historical events and would not be too strict if I have failed to give the exact dates. I do admit, History as an MA subject is far more difficult than International Relations. I have of course not dared to write my real views about some of our illustrious rulers from the past and have written only what I read in the course books. I couldn't take the risk of failing the exam by writing what I really feel about many historical events. I had a reputation to keep, which was much enhanced by a radio program telecast on a local FM station about my educational qualifications achieved from the dark dungeon of the death cell. Thank God, the presenter who did the program had never visited the prison to know that it was not actually so dark, and was not a cave but resembled a small study room. I was not aware of the program but was watching *Khabarnama* (9 p.m. News) much to the annoyance of my Haandi Waals and inmates in my part of the barrack. I learned about it the next day. Even one of the wardens mentioned that I had now become a real celebrity; having my name mentioned in the popular program without writing a letter is no small thing, I learnt.

Except on very rare occasions, every day I spent in the death cell was more or less the same, but in the barrack everyday is a new day. Before I knew, the holy month of Ramadan arrived. My last five Ramadan spent in the death cell always exhausted me. Now for the first time in my life I enjoyed the month. Waking up early in the morning and smelling the aroma of *Sehri* (meal taken at the dawn during ramadan) being prepared gave the day a kick-start. Even the rowdier inmates were at their best behavior. I also got a visit from Papa and for the first time after five years, he did not shake hands because the meeting took place across the double iron meshing of the visiting room. We had difficulty in hearing each other in the noisy room, small price to pay for a new life. On the 29th of Ramadan, everybody started waiting for the verdict of *Ruet-i-Hilal* Committee (the moon-sighting committee). As soon as it was announced that the moon had not been sighted there were loud 'ooohs' and 'aaahs', as if Shahid Afridi had been bowled out first ball. Some wondered aloud why the government never appointed any younger people who had better eyesight for moon sighting. Some could not understand why the Ramadan moon was always sighted and the Eid moon was never. There was also a group of "scientists", who disputed the American claim of landing on the moon. If we could not sight it properly how could they land on it, they opined.

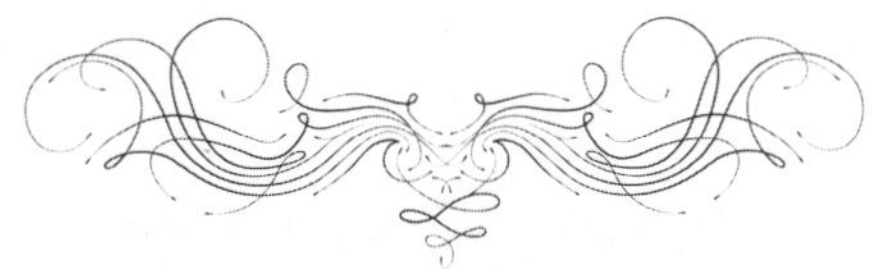

CHAPTER 13

REFLECTIONS; THE WAIT TO BE RELEASED

"Life isn't about waiting for the storm to pass. It is about dancing in the rain."

I was living in a paradise of happiness, where the word sorrow was unheard of. There were emotional early morning scenes when almost everybody excluding me, wept a little remembering the Eid days they had spent with families and friends. I had completely forgotten how I had spent the Eid in my other life. I just felt sorry at seeing them with tears in their eyes. The Eid prayers are offered in the ground of the sector, which is the biggest ground in the prison and where the whole population of the prison including the wardens and officers unlucky to be on duty, would offer their prayers. Eid days are the only days when the gates of the juvenile sector are opened for the "general public (older prisoners)" who come to offer the Eid prayers. Many of them sought me out and praised me, saying they had heard about me on the radio or read in the newspapers.

The four holidays of Eid are one of the most important days in the life of prisoners, especially the younger ones. These are the only days when cassette and CD players are allowed, and what a melodious noise they create. Imagine two or three big decks playing different songs at their full volume. One had to shout while speaking to someone sitting on the same bench. I must have drank liters of tea and soft drink, and eaten kilos of *mithai* (sweetmeats) of every kind, besides the traditional *Sawayyan* (vermicelli), *Chaat* (fruit salad), *Pakoras*, and *Samosas*. I could feel the pressure of being a celebrity. I was invited to many tea parties and had to attend each of them lest I be declared an arrogant bookworm. After three days of this blissful madness everything retured to normal.

The day starts at 6:30 a.m. when the first bugle of the day is sounded. Walking in the fresh early morning breeze gives me a pleasure I cannot describe. It is one of the many blessings I enjoy now after five years of solitary confinement and deprivation. I take a bath in one of the two bathrooms located at one end of the barrack. After breakfast, Rafiq and I go to the school as teachers. I teach the FA (History) to 12 young prisoners. I enjoy their respect not just because I am their teacher, more educated or spent more time in jail, but also because I am older than them. Rafiq has the more difficult task of teaching basic ABCs to the illiterate prisoners.

A Library and Computer Education Center with the aid of an NGO has been established for the juvenile prisoners. I have also taken admission in the Computer Center and can now do some basic activities on the computer. We are allowed to play games on the PC when the Center Incharge, an employee of the NGO, is in a good mood. These games are more interesting and perhaps better than the ones I used to play at the video games shop. But they are also more complex and not as exciting as the *Street Fighter*, of which I was the undisputed champion. After computer classes, I go back to the barrack and help my Haandi Waals prepare lunch. Then I take a walk and play badminton. I sometimes play cricket too and have the same problems faced by the Pakistani fast bowlers; too many wides and no-balls. My batting is like Shahid Afridi, but I cannot hit any fours and sixes. Being the most respected prisoner does not make the bowlers bowl any slower to me. Reading books and responding to letters, or listening to the radio takes away the rest of my day. Owning one of the two television sets in the barrack does not mean I can veto the majority and watch the Current Affairs programs. I have to join the rest in watching the dramas, some of which, especially the comedy programs, are actually quite interesting.

An appeal has been filed by the father of the deceased against the commutation of the death sentence to life imprisonment. I will be released around five years from now taking into account the various remissions granted to prisoners by the President, Chief Minister, IG Prisons and credit gained for acquiring educational qualification. We have also filed appeals before the Supreme Court seeking our acquittal.

I have seen death very closely for five years and spent every single night thinking about it. I do not fear death itself, but

I do not want to die with a noose around my neck. Having experienced the joys of life and its pleasures, I fear the death cell. I am sometimes seized by the fear that this dream may end as suddenly as it started. I have come to love Allah, for the mysterious ways His hand moves. I request Him to make pleasant the remaining surprises of my life. The beauty of life can be best understood by loving and enjoying the small things.

My life is a living example, that anything may happen to anybody at any time, and that miracles do happen, though we tend to overlook them. Everyone has dreams, that can be turned into reality. Sometimes we have hopes which we know are impossible to attain. However, one still creates a dreamworld to find an escape from realities. It is purely for their entertainment value that dreams are the greatest gift a human is blessed with. Miracles are the happening of events which we can never think to dream of. There is a long list of people who played a part in changing my life for the better, but most of all I am grateful to the jail.

Thank you, Jail for providing excellent educational facilities. The accommodation was not too bad either. You taught me to take pleasure in the small things in life. Because of you, I have met and come into contact with wonderful, kind-hearted and real human beings. I am still enjoying the show, but I request you to please let me go now, so that I may start my third life and write the final chapter of my book.

EPILOGUE

"Don't let the darkness of the past cover the brightness of the future."

Somebody truly said, "It is not what happens to me that matters, but how I behave while it is happening." Sohail Fida's behavior despite the grossly unpleasant and inhuman event, was exemplary and remarkable. He is undoubtedly made of very tough stuff. He will hopefully be a free man in less than a year, and while he is looking forward to start his 'third life' as he calls it. He is at the same time apprehensive, as to how he will adjust to the future new-found freedom. One can understand his fears, because he has become accustomed to the life in jail, especially now that he has moved to 'B' class in jail. It will not be easy to go from near solitude and a restricted routine to absolute freedom and the crowd. There will be too many people from his family and friends, and even strangers, who will want to listen to his story and form varying opinions. Being released from prison will not remove the inherent accusation for which he was sentenced to death. There will be many skeptics. It will be awkward, facing the relatives and friends of the boy he was accused of murdering, especially the father of the deceased. It will be imperative, that he continues to fight and establish himself through his sincere actions and becomes what he loves most, a contributor to good of society. Whatever might happen after Sohail Fida is released, it will not give him back the years that he lost and which in all probability was due to no fault of his. One feels that the verdict was wrong and possibly manipulated, but that is now history. Erasing the stigma by good deeds is what Sohail Fida and all his well-wishers would hope and want. His conduct throughout his confinement and torture has been one of exceptional goodness and legendary grit and resilience. He has never shown even the slightest bitterness towards those who tortured him into submission and a forced confession. Only in passing has he mentioned the neglect in duty and rules of the court doctor and magistrate in the procedure for recording his statement. It is a rare strength of character when a man carries no revengeful feelings. His behavior, in absolute dire circumstances is truly commendable, and while Sohail Fida deserves great respect for this, much of the credit rightly belongs to his parents, especially his grandfather, who inculcated those traits during his early years, whereby he brought out the inherent goodness and determination in adversity. The same characteristics will be needed with the similar tenacity and value-driven courage to purposefully establish his life out of jail.

Imagine the high thinking of this truly noble soul that he has already envisioned multi-educational projects once out of jail. It will be his endeavor to set up schools in every jail of the country. This chain of schools will be simply called 'Jail School' and will enroll juvenile inmates of the jails. We hope that many philanthropists, NGOs and even the government will help him to realize his singular ambition in life after his term in jail ends. One is forced to think, that such a man cannot be involved in the heinous crime for which he was convicted. And that is why, it is our hope and prayer that he will finally receive justice and the stigma against his name will be erased for ever. Amen.

Wing Commander (Retired)
Hadi Rizvi

Annexure 'A'
Sohail Fida's Life at a Glance

List of Important Events in Sohail Fida's Life

Name:	Sohail Fida
Hometown:	Mingora, Swat
Date of Birth:	28th August 1982
Admission in College:	September 1999
Under Police Custody:	02nd April 2000
Transferred to District Jail, Swat:	13th April 2000
Passed FA Exams (12th year of Education):	2002
Sentenced to Death by Session Judge, Swat:	23rd July 2002
Transferred to Central Prison, Haripur:	27th July 2002
Passed BA Exams (14th year of Education):	2004
Passed MA (International Relations) Exams:	2006
Death Sentence Commuted to Life Imprisonment:	27th July 2007
Transfer to Juvenile Sector:	August 2007

Promoted to 'B' Class:	June 2008
Passed MA (History) Exams:	2008
Appeared in MA (English Literature) Exams:	2011
Expected Result for MA (Eng. Lit.) Exams:	March 2012

Annexure 'B'
Sohail Fida's Life in Pictures

Sohail Fida (left) with his sister, Salma Fida

Sohail Fida (right) with his sister, Laila Fida
01-02-1987

Sohail Fida

Sohail Fida near Atoo Bridge, Khyber Pakhtunkhwa

Sohail Fida (left) & his younger brother, Shiraz Fida on Shiraz's birthday

Sohail Fida

Sohail Fida & Shiraz Fida in Murree 1997

Sohail Fida with his Grandfather, Daaji
September 1999

Sohail Fida
March 2000

May 2002

Sohail Fida under Police Custody

Sohail Fida (right) with his father and his niece, Sarah on a visit while Sohail appears for F.A. Exams in 2002

Sohail Fida sharing a light moment with his father (left) in May 2002

With Haripur Nazim (Mayor of Haripur), Yousaf Ayub Khan (first from the right), who is the grandson of President Ayub Khan in 2008

Sohail Fida in 'B' Class cell on Human Rights Day 2010

With Federal Secretary of Law and Justice on Human Rights Day 2010

Sohail Fida (right) with his co-accused cousin, M. Rafiq

Rafiq in 'B' Class cell on
Human Rights Day 2010

Sohail Fida in 'B' Class Cell
2011

In front of the Computer Center for Juvenile Prisoners

Studying for MA (History) Exams

Annexure 'C'
Correspondence

A clearer interpretation of the letter is present after this original reproduction.

Sultan Muhammad Khan
Former Foreign Secretary

91-B/1, Khayaban-e-Shahbaz,
Phase VII, D.H.A.,
Karachi-75500.
Tel : (0092-21) 5855529

10th Aug 07

Dear Mr. Fida

Your letter to Mr. Muhammad Ali Khan of Paramount has been reproduced in the Book Section of the DAWN dated 5th August 07. It must have been seen by a few thousand people, and I hope will lead to positive developments. A copy is enclosed.

I want to thank you for your kind words about my book. I am deeply impressed by your dedication to learning and [illegible] of knowledge. Your achievments are all the more commendable, considering the circumstances in which you are placed.

I do not know the what and why of the events that have placed you on the death row, but I am by conviction opposed to death penalty and my sympathies and prayers are with you.

I am sending you today by separate Regd. postal mail two books.

(1) Back to the Pavilion by (late) Gen. Atiqur Rahman and (2) Heart to Heart by Natwar Singh

3

-3-

ltan Muhammad Khan
Former Foreign Secretary

91-B/1, Khayaban-e-Shahbaz,
Phase VII, D.H.A.,
Karachi-75500.
Tel : (0092-21) 5855529

If you are interested in any particular book please write to me

Wishing you lots and lots of luck,

Sincerely yours
Sultan Mohammad Khan

10th Aug 2007

Dear Mr. Fida,

Your letter to Mr. Muhammad Ali Khan of Paramount has been re-produced in the Book section of the DAWN dated 5th August 2007. It must have been seen by a few thousand people and I hope it will lead to positive developments. A copy is closed.

I want to thank you for your kind words about my book. I am deeply impressed by your dedication to learning and pursuit of knowledge. Your achievements are all the more commendable considering the circumstance in which you are placed.

I do not know the what and why of the events that have placed you on the death row, but I am by conviction opposed to death penalty, and my sympathies and prayers are with you.

I am sending you today by separate Registered Postal Mail two books:

i. Back to Pavilion by (Late) Gen. Atiqur Rehman, and
ii. Heart to Heart by Natwar Singh

If you are interested in any particular book, please write to me.

Wishing you lots and lots of luck.

Sincerely yours,

Sultan Muhammad Khan

FINANCIAL POST

Dated:-09-10-2007

Dear Sohail Fida,

After reading your two letters in the Dawn book review i was deeply moved and wrote to Mr. Muhammad Ali khan who has given me your postal address so that we communicate personally. I would be very interested in publishing your story as part of a serial over the weeks to come. I am, however, concerned about your access to postal services (would you be able to get someone to mail the letters to me?) or would you like to communicate through some other means? If you are able to post your letters please do send me your story and i will publish it in installments. I will also send you any feedback I might receive about your story.

I look forward to hearing from you. A very happy Eid to you, and may Allah give you the faith and strength to surpass all these hurdles placed before you and be a free man soon.

Best regards,

Qudsia Kadri
C.E.O & Editor-in-Chief,
Daily financial Post,
106/c 11th commercial street, Phase 2 extension
DHA
Karachi
pakistan

Head Office: 106/C 11th Commercial Street, Phase II Ext. D.H.A., Karachi, Pakistan.
Telephone: 92-21 5381626, Fax: 5802760. E-mail: fpost@dancom3.com.pk, Website: www.dailyfpost.com

Dy.No.251/2008-DG(SD)
Government of Pakistan
Ministry of Social Welfare and Special Education
Opposite NORI Hospital, G.8/4
****

Director General(SD)
Phone: 051-9263274

Islamabad, the 13th February 2008.

Subject:- **RECOMMENDATION FOR PROVISION OF B-CLASS FOR MR. SOHAIL FIDA S/O FIDA HUSSAIN IMPRISONED AT CENTRAL JAIL, HAIRPUR.**

Dear

It was learnt that Mr. Sohail Fida S/O Fida Hussain, convicted under Section 302 at the age of 17 years, has been imprisoned in the Central Jail, Haripur for the last eight years. Subsequently, the undersigned and Director, National Commission for Child Welfare & Development visited Central Jail, Haripur and met Mr. Sohail Fida in the office of Malik Fakhr-e-Alam, Superintendent Jail. It was informed that Mr. Sohail Fida did Matric, F.A, B.A and M.A.(IR, History) during his imprisonment. He has developed good behaviour and rendering remarkable services in the areas of teaching and improving the conduct of fellow prisoners. He is regular columnist of Financial Post and photocopies of his articles are enclosed.

2. In view of foregoing, it is strongly recommended that Mr. Sohail Fida may be considered for provision of B-Class in the Jail, if permissible under the jail manual.

With regards,

Yours sincerely,

(Muhammad Javed Alam)

Mr. Fazal-ur-Rehman
Inspector General Prisons,
Government of NWFP,
Peshawar

CC to:-
1. Senior Superintendent, Central Jail Haripur.
2. Mr. Sohail Fida S/O Fida ~~Mohsin~~ Hussain, Central Jail Hariupur.

ON THE BEHALF OF BARRISTER SHAHIDA SAHIL

Jan 14, 2008

Home Secretary
Government of NWFP
Civil Secretariat
Peshawar
Fax No: 091-9210201

Information:
Human Rights Commission of Pakistan
House No. 25, Street No.1, New Town,
Opposite Gul Haji Plaza, University Road Peshawar
Fax No: 091-5853318

Subject: **Request to Grant "B" Class to Mr. Sohail Fida, Undergoing Life Sentence in Central Jail Haripure Hazara**

Sir,

The case of Mr. Sohail Fida for grant of "B" class in Central Jail Haripur is pending before the government of N.W.F.P. Human Rights Commission of Pakistan has followed Mr. Sohail Fida's case with keen interest. According to available information he is a talented young man who needs to be appreciated for his pursuit of education and maintenance of good behaviour during imprisonment. From the prison cell he has successfully continued his education and his outstanding achievement was attainment of 7th position in M.A. International Relation from Hazara University.

Mr. Sohail Fida belongs to an educated and responsible business family of Swat. His father besides social-community work in engaged is petroleum business M/S FIDA PETROLEUM, G.T. ROAD Rah.... Abad Mingora, Swat.

Due to Mr. Sohail Fida's abiding interest in education and good behaviour he is commended by the prison staff and fellow convicts.

In view of his educational accomplishment, good behaviour and social status of his family, Human Rights Commission of Pakistan appeals to you to kindly grant Mr. Sohail Fida "B" Class in Haripur Central Jail, Haripur. This would enable him to continue his intellectual and educational pursuits in conducive environments.

We thank you for your consideration and look forward to early issue of necessary order.

Sincerely yours,

Brig Rao Abid Hamid
Coordinator
Vulnerable prisoners project
Human Rights Commission of Pakistan

Aiwan-i-Jamhoor, 107-Tipu Block, New Garden Town, Lahore-54600
Tel:(92)(42) 5864994, 5838341, 5865969 ■ Fax (92)(42) 5883582
■ E-Mail: hrcp@hrcp-web.org ■ Website: www.hrcp-web.org

No 171 /2/Judl: Dated 16 /4/2008

For Sohail Fida

From: The District Officer,
Revenue & Estates/
Collector, Swat.

To: The Section Officer(Prisons),
Government of N.W.F.P. Home &
Tribal Affairs Deptt: Peshawar.

Subject:- GRANT OF B-CLASS.

Memo:

Reference your Office letter No.4/41-SO(Prs)HD/07 dated 11.01.2008 and No.4/41-SO(Prs)/07 V-9 dated 01.03.2008 on the subject noted above.

In this context, copies of the following educational documents in respect of convict Prisoner namely Sohail Fida furnished by the Tehsildar, Babozai District Swat are sent herewith.

1. D.M.C. of M.A. History.
2. Provisional Certificate of International, MA Relation.
3. Provisional Certificate of B.A.

According to the enclosed Affadavit of father of the convict prisoner, the original Degrees of M.A. and B.A. have not been issued by the concerned Universities as yet. As regards the land record in the name of petitioner/convict prisoner, the Tehsildar, Babozai has reported that the convict Prisoner Sohail Fida has got no landed property in his name in the Revenue record please.

Enclo:(~~05~~ 14).

DISTRICT OFFICER
REVENUE & ESTATES/COLLECTOR
SWAT.

B/C

GOVERNMENT OF N.-W.F.P.
HOME & T.As. DEPARTMENT.
No. 4141-SO(Prs)HD/07 V-(9)
Dated Peshawar, the 16-5-2008

To

The Inspector General of Prisons,
NWFP Peshawar.

Subject:- <u>GRANT OF B-CLASS.</u>

Dear Sir,

I am directed to refer to your letter NO.3167/WE, dated 29/12/2008 on the subject noted above and to convey that the Competent Authority has been pleased to allow B-Class to the convicted prisoner Sohail Fida S/O Fida Hussain, presently confined in Central Prison Haripur.

2- You are requested to kindly take further necessary action in the matter at the earliest.

Yours faithfully,

(MAQSOOD PERVEZ)
SECTION OFFICER (PRISONS).

Endrst: of even No/date.

Copy forwarded to Superintendent Central Prison Haripur for similar necessary action.

16/5/2008
SECTION OFFICER (PRISONS).

2110
26-5-08

DIET SCALE OF B.CLASS PRISONER.

RULE 260.

Name of item	Diet scale for meat eaters
Wheat Atta	583 gram
Dal	117 gram
Meat	175 gram
Milk	233 gram
Milk	117 gram
Vegetable Ghee	29 gram
Sugar	58 gram
Tea	29 gram
Vegetable	117 gram
Potatoes	117 gram
Condiments	15 gram (Chilies 06 gram+Garlic 06 gram+Turmeric 03 gram)
Salt	15 gram
Fire Wood	886 gram

+ 16 eggs on monthly bases

Now, gas

SUPERINTENDENT
CENTRAL PRISON HARIPUR.

FINANCIAL POST Monday, April 13, 2009

The forgotten prisoner

Qudsia Kadri

The Financial Post published a series of stories in November 2007, which continued to appear till January 2009. The series was an account of the life of Sohail Fida, who has bravely faced his imprisonment days in the Haripur jail, since the past many years. Sohail was imprisoned at the age of 17 in a false blind murder case. Sohail has bravely faced all his ordeals in prison, his five years in the death cell, from where he courageously faced the long, endless nights and completed his masters in International Relations, attaining a 7th position from Hazara University.

He continues now to serve his remaining period of life imprisonment, and has completed his double M.A in history this year. Today Sohail has an added feather in his educational qualifications. He has cleared his double master's degree in History and has secured the 5th position in the Hazara University. Receiving Sohail's hand written letters along with his story has been a pleasant, rewarding and sad experience for me. His courage, his perseverance, his insight and positive attitude has helped us appreciate the small things in life. It has confirmed our belief of the injustice, victimization, callousness and corruption prevalent and rampant in our system.

What has jolted us time and again remind the Pakistani society is the injustice and total lack of fair play, compassion and humanity as far as the common man of this nation is concerned.

Unfortunately, over the past two year I have written several times to various Governors of NWFP. From Mr. Aurekzai, to Mr. Owais Ghani and now to Mr. Amir Khan Hoti, no response has ever been given. Except a letter from the Governor's secretariat in February 2008, during the tenure of Mr. Aurekzai, which was signed by some section officer who had not bothered to go through the proper records of the jail and whatever information was provided by the Haripur jail authorities were passed on to me.

But the interesting aspect of that letter was that remissions in the sentence of Sohail Fida has only been 37 months and 10 days remission. From April 2000 when he was arrested to April 2009, Sohail's remission seems unbelievable, the fact that he has earned such a minimal period, goes against the very essence of the fact that Sohail was arrested soon after he had taken admission in collage, he completed 2 year of intermediate, 2 years of a bachelor's degree (B.A), 2 years of Master's (M.A) in International Relations, and now 2 years of double M.A in History! Indeed quite a record, which most of us living in freedom, breathing fresh air and enjoying our much loved free world, have failed to achieve.

Education the most important ingredient, for living a reasonably good life, with an understanding of what a moderate way of life is, coupled with lots of hard work, commitment and dedication, which is totally missing in Pakistan. Literacy and education have been erased from the books of successive governments. We hear a lot of rhetoric, speeches and seminars on a routine basis, emphasizing on literacy, but it all seems like a sad joke in Pakistan today. And when a young man turns his tragic experience after falling prey to a corrupt police system, an unjust & partial rule of law, he instead of bemoaning his fate, turns to books, turns to broadening his mind and gaining knowledge, which no one shall ever take away from him - he is unfortunately, today still behind the dark cells of prison.

In a country where corruption is the name of the game, where powerful contacts and trunks full of cash can attain every wish, where a 'genie' or a Godfather is always near-by to clean up the mess. Sohail Fida and many others like him stand out for their courage, their belief, their positive acceptance of their fate. It's time that young men and women like Sohail are brought back into this corrupt society of the nation, they are the real heroes, they are the people whom the present and coming generations can actually look upto.

It is time that the government of Pakistan, of NWFP, the judiciary and the Honorable Chief Justice of Pakistan take immediate note of Sohail Fida Hussain, and I am sure thousand like him who are locked in the prisons of Pakistan since years & years.

Our sadness, our tears, our pain after cases like Sohail come up, are minute. The tragedy his mother, his brothers, his father and his sisters have been suffering since the past almost 9 years is unexplainable. Every time I have spoken to Mr. Fida Hussain, Sohails father, his voice, his "never giving up" attitude makes me feel ashamed as to the enormity of grieve they have been through as a family, yet have managed to look up in hope, every time anything positive no matter how small has come up. Be it Sohail being granted a better class in jail (must mention Ms. Sadia Sarwar, Additional Home Secretary NWFP, who was extremely helpful and kind, when I had spoken to her a year ago and explained the entire case to her). Fida Hussain's voice was full of joy when he phoned me to inform us about Sohail's latest success in his double M.A results.

Its time the Honorable Chief Justice took note of such cases (our expectations from the government is none). Sohail has served most part of his life imprisonment sentence, it is pertinent to note that he is also entitled for the I.G prison's and the NWFP government's and Governor's/Chief Minister's remission, which became due in July 2008.

Let us hope & pray Sohail's dream to publish a book shall soon become a reality and his experience will help others in similar situations to take control of their sorrows and hardships. We, at Financial Post are grateful, that we got the opportunity to publish Sohail's story and we will continue to pursue his genuine case till Sohail gains his independence and is able to once again breathe the fresh air of freedom.

Visit our website www.dailyf-post.com for the series of Sohail Fida's story

CERTIFICATE OF APPRECIATION

REGIONAL DIRECTORATE OF HUMAN RIGHTS PESHAWAR

Regional Directorate of Human Rights and Save the Children

Sweden proudly presents the Certificate of Appreciation

to Mr. Sohail Fida, Juvenile School Teacher for 5 yrs *on* 17/11/2011

for exemplary services to the project

"Rehabilitation of Juvenile Prisoners."

Muhammad Saimen
Director
Regional Directorate
of Human Rights

Khizar Shah
Syed Khizar Ali Shah
Deputy Director
Regional Directorate
of Human Rights